THE MIND OF MASTERY

R.O.A.R.

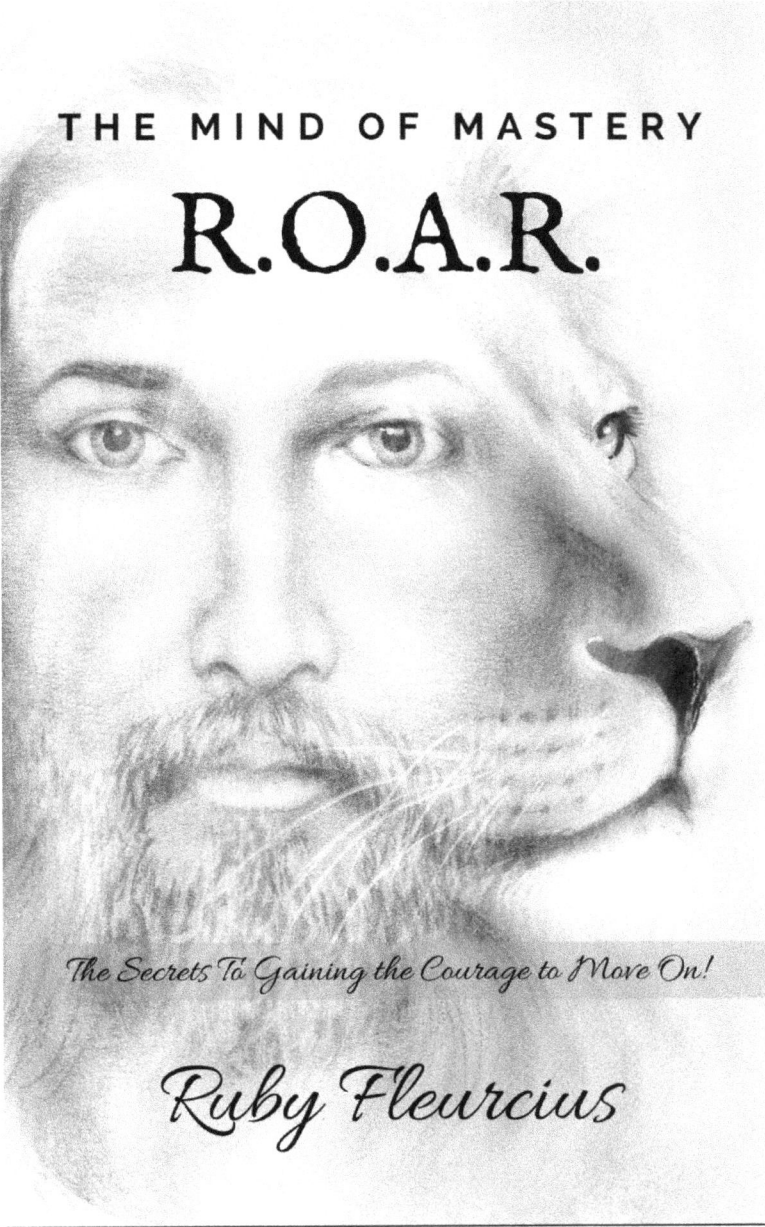

The Secrets To Gaining the Courage to Move On!

Ruby Fleurcius

The Mind of Mastery R.O.A.R.
The Secrets To Gaining the Courage to Move On!

Spiritually Fit Publications
Ruby Fleurcius
581 N. Park Ave. Ste. #725
Apopka, FL 32704
321-312-0744

Published in the United States of America

ISBN: 978-0-9990900-2-2
$19.95

The Mind of Mastery R.O.A.R.
The Secrets To Gaining the Courage to Move On!

Spiritually Fit Publications
Ruby Fleurcius
581 N. Park Ave. Ste. #725
Apopka, FL 32704
321-312-0744

Published in the United States of America

ISBN: 978-0-9990900-2-2
$19.95

Table of Contents

DEDICATION..7

INTRODUCTION..9

CHAPTER 1 13

    THE 80/20 R.O.A.R. 13

CHAPTER 2 45

    YOUR ROARING CIRCLE.......................................45

CHAPTER 3 69

    THE DON'T GET CAUGHT ROAR! 69

CHAPTER 4 81

    THE ROARING WAD...81

CHAPTER 5 109

    RELATIONSHIP WISDOM ROAR..........................109

CHAPTER 6 125

    DOORMAT OF DISGUISE ROAR 125

CHAPTER 7 133

    THE UNCOMMON FREEDOM ROAR 133

CHAPTER 8 147

    THE ROARING MIND GERM................................147

CHAPTER 9 159

    THE ROARING CHEATER FROM WITHIN 159

CHAPTER 10 ....**175**

THE RIGHT A WRONG ROAR.. 175

CHAPTER 11..**193**

THE VUJÁ DÉ ROAR... 193

CHAPTER 12 ....**199**

ROARING KRYPTONITE 199

CHAPTER 13 ....**217**

SWEET TEMPTATION ROAR 217

CHAPTER 14 .... **223**

THE MIND OF MASTERY R.O.A.R.. 223

CHAPTER 15 ....**231**

THE HAPPINESS ROAR... 231

CHAPTER 16 ....**241**

ROARING TRUTH 241

CHAPTER 17 .... **279**

GROW GREAT.. 279

DEDICATION

I would like to dedicate this book to all of those who are seeking to understand the hidden truths about relationship awareness. We envision the perfect fairytale home or fairytale relationship, and I wish that for everyone as well; but, what do we do when it becomes a living nightmare? Hopefully, that is not the case; but, it is you that I dedicate this book to. I reach into the depths of my soul to pull out hope and restoration for you; I have been where you are. I was once blind to reality, not because I could not see; it was that I did not want to see. I could not bear the pain of my little empire crashing down if I opened my eyes—until that one day came that I had to stop lying to myself. I had to stop lying to life, I had to stop lying to God, I had to begin to own my life, and I had to begin to learn the types of people that I needed to avoid in order to protect my sanity. I would also like to thank everyone who contributed to the experiences that gave me the inspiration to write this book "**The Mind of Mastery R.O.A.R.**." To God be the Glory. Amen.

INTRODUCTION

It's a relationship phenomenon going on; it's so easy to pick up a date, jump into a relationship, get our sex on, or get married. It would be fair for me to say that it is not the money, it is not the car, it is not the house, and it is not our status that keeps our relationships intact. Although they are nice to have, but we must understand that all of those things are fleeting because as soon as the newness wears off, reality sets in. And, off we go to the next best thing...... If we choose not to get a grip in advance, we will find ourselves saying, "I don't understand why he or she is leaving me?" If we find ourselves asking that question, then it would be obvious that we have associated power, money, sex, or status into the equation of a failing relationship. This book, "The Mind of Mastery R.O.A.R. " opens our mind to the reality of what's really going on in a relationship that we are totally oblivious to. In my opinion, our NORM has left room for neglect; especially when we think that everything is all hunky-dory; and, the woman or man on the other end is coming in for the ultimate take-over that we cannot see coming because we are too blinded by our selfish wants and needs. Most often, we keep our private life behind closed doors, but I want to open up some doors to show what's really happening in the real world to ensure that adjustments on our behalf can be made in advance to ensure that we do not become an innocent victim.

In a relationship, we have all been thrown under the bus at some point. For me, I have definitely had my share of encounters—I have been dogged out, rejected, abused, cheated on, sold out, etc. You name it—it has happened; but, I have not allowed it to stop me. I believe in creating a win-win situation out of everything, and don't be surprised if you read about it in one of these treacherous relationship stories. However, there are many different reasons why someone would throw us under the bus or why we would throw someone under the bus as well. Before I move on, let me explain the colloquialism, "Thrown under the Bus." It simply means to betray, blame, reject, or disown; which in my opinion, is based solely upon one's perception of the situation, circumstance, or event that may have led up to this FEELING of being thrown under the bus. Although, it may or may not have been the intent or motive of who caused the atrocity; but, it should give us enough willpower to weed through the types of people to avoid the next time around.

When we allow our mind to be led astray by our emotions, we will find that we will become extra sensitive about everything—we will think that people are talking about us, we will think that people are laughing at us, we will think that people are judging us, we will think that people don't like us, we will think that everyone is out to get us, we will think that someone is trying to take advantage of us, we will think that everyone has an agenda, and the list goes on. This is how the mind will set a trap for us so that we can wallow in our unchecked negative emotions; and if we do not strengthen ourselves mentally and emotionally, we will easily break physically. When this happens, it's revealed through uncontrollable behavior such as outbursts of anger, temper tantrums, yelling, screaming, fussing, fighting, attitude problems, the inability to control what comes out of our mouth, or downright hatefulness. As life would have it, we will all feel as if someone has thrown us under the bus from time-to-time; however, we must get the facts first, be quick to forgive, do not burn any bridges, learn what types of people to avoid, and move on. This is not a matter of being prejudice; it's a matter of being wise—it is written all over the Book of Proverbs regarding what types of people to associate ourselves with; yet, it goes right over our head day in and day out. When our relationship is in turmoil, it is common to look for a miracle to come from someone else outside of ourselves; but, I believe that our miracle is within us. We often pray for God to send someone to help us, opposed to praying for God to help us to help ourselves. He reveals all that we need to know; but for some odd reason, we choose to go by the opinions of others when our answer is right before us in plain sight. When we need to avoid someone, we know it within the depths of our soul; yet, we ignore it. Only to become hurt, rejected, abused, or betrayed by the one that we knew that we should have exercised caution with anyway. Besides, we do not really kick ourselves because of what they did to us; we kick ourselves because we did not listen to the voice from within.

If one has a desire to become, achieve, and do more in life, do not hold on to drama, it is a distraction—it holds us back from fulfilling the desires of our heart. If someone does not want to be a part of our circle, we cannot force them—so find people who are NOT vengeful, envious, and cruel that does not mind being a part of the empire that we are trying to build. Take it from me; it is not good to surround ourselves with people, places, and things that are always tearing our kingdom down—if we want all that God has to offer us; we need to surround ourselves with KINGDOM BUILDERS who are not ashamed to build their lives one brick at a time. I need you to get from under the bus, and pick up a brick— it's time to start rebuilding the Empire that's already hidden inside of you.

The *Roar of Mastery* is engrained in those who do not settle for defeat, those who find a way out of no way, those who set a guard over their mind, those who invest into their well-being, those who are willing to put away their abrasiveness, and those who are willing to do what others are not willing to do. The roar of this type of person will tackle problems head-on without running away from the issues of their past, present, or future.

The *Mental Roaring* of those who are well-invested can be heard without this person saying ONE word....this type of ROAR is King, but it is as humble as a little lamb. This type of ROAR marks its mental territory by becoming a Master over oneself mentally, emotionally, physically, and spiritually. This type of R.O.A.R. will **R**espect themselves and others, it will **O**vercome obstacles, it will **A**chieve more than the average person, and it will **R**each back to help others. As a part of the "The *Mind Of Mastery R.O.A.R.,*" there we have it—the ROAR is **R**espect, **O**vercome, **A**chieve, and **R**each. Rest assured that our strength can easily be found when we have our emotions and mind under control with an irrevocable desire to succeed in the workplace or in our personal lives.

CHAPTER 1

The 80/20 R.O.A.R.

Relationships are all around us; we can't get away from them; therefore, we must learn how to choose them carefully. Our goal is to become an asset and not a liability in a relationship; and in order to become that, we must understand the value of who we are, why we are, and what we are. If we do not understand that, we will begin to become a liability to those who do not find value in who we are or what we have to offer. In a solid relationship, it's hard to get rid of an asset, but it's very easy to get rid of a liability—so, we must provide some form of substance that's irreplaceable in a relationship that's worth having, keeping, or pursuing.

Now, the question is, "Does true love really exist?" The answer is "YES!" There are times when we feel that true love has eluded us; but the truth is, true love resides within us. In a relationship, like attracts like. If we do not truly love ourselves unselfishly, we will find that we unknowingly drive away the people who are making an attempt to extend his or her love toward us; and, attract those who contribute to the hurt. Therefore, it is not that love doesn't exist; it is a matter of whether we reject or embrace the love that's coming our way. If we are not sure how to love, then we need to learn—it's okay to pick up a book or take a class on love. If we have never experienced love, then we need to find it within ourselves first, by making a list of the good/bad things, positive/negative things, or the right/wrong things about ourselves, as well as the fears that we have that prevents us from loving ourselves and others. If we want true love, we must be willing to give it; but, in order to give it, we must possess it—we cannot drink from a well that's all dried up.

In this book, I am going to show you how to forget about the hurts, pains, and reservations that you may have about love. So what, if you have been hurt—don't let it take what truly belongs to you, and that is your right to be happy. Once you learn to recognize the types of people to avoid, you will be able to love like you have never been hurt before. And, you will also be able to heal beyond all human understanding as your well begins to overflow in good relationships; therefore, quenching the thirst for true love to replace it with confidence.

The simplest way to develop confidence is to believe in oneself without becoming frustrated by the opinions of others. However, the lack of confidence will cause the best of us to use everything and everyone as an excuse why we are not taking action or why we are not succeeding in certain areas. For that reason, we must know and understand our challenges or limits to ensure that we are able to design an action plan to work on them or to work through them. This will definitely enable us to turn our limitations and challenges into opportunities. I believe that there is no limit to what we can achieve when we are confident that we know our stuff, especially when building quality relationships.

When dealing with the matters of the heart, there are times when we cannot help who we love; however, in the midst of loving, we can control who we AVOID! In dealing with different types of relationships, there are a lot of people that will make it to the avoid list; however, there are a lot of people that we need to keep at arm's length as well. Plus, there are certain people that we cannot just get rid of, such as family members, coworkers, etc.; therefore, we must learn how to deal with difficult people. Although, no one is perfect, and we stand to be corrected ourselves; therefore, we must operate on the Relationship 80/20 Rule. That means that a person must exhibit 80% or more of the positive characteristics and 20% or less of the negative characteristics that we can live with, in order to remain in our inner circle. If one cannot live with a characteristic trait that falls in that 20% negative category, leave them alone…….there may be a few characteristics that are unacceptable or fall in the zero tolerance category. However, one must decide what characteristics fall into that category—do not compromise if that is a sore spot or vice; but, under no circumstance does one need to mistreat anyone regarding a negative characteristic, politely move on. If one desire a relationship based on 70/30, 60/40, 50/50, 40/60, etc. rest assured that there will be a decline in the quality of that relationship, and it may not be a pretty picture. The lower we decline on the positive characteristics, the more we are settling or compromising, and the more issues that we will have to wrestle with.

Once we understand that no one is exempt from problems, issues, and losses, we are better able to embrace our faith with an inner knowing that all things will work together for our good. If we look around us right now, we will see that we are blessed; but, for some odd reason, we can't seem to embrace or understand our blessings. So we keep looking around for something or someone that will only keep us feeling aloof, looking for our next quick-fix. Most often the scales on our eyes or our selfishness prevents us from seeing our relationships clearly; therefore causing our blessings not to appear as blessings. Our greatest potential in relationships is wrapped up in our attitude. It is the one thing that will measure that in which is immeasurable, and creates a relationship of endless possibilities, if it is positive.

Listen to me, if we have enough faith to allow a negative attitude to rule and reign in our lives, it is fair to say that we have enough faith to allow God to change our negative attitude into a positive one; besides, in my opinion, it takes the same amount of energy. The simplest way to develop confidence in our positive mental attitude is to believe in oneself, without becoming frustrated by the opinions of others. On the other hand, the lack of confidence will cause the best of us to use everything and everyone as an excuse regarding why we are not taking action, why we are not succeeding in certain areas, why we are failing in our relationship, or why we are engaging ourselves in unequally yoked behavior.

1st Type of Person to Avoid

Avoid People Who Are Unequally Yoked With You

Fear is the primary culprit of unequally yoked relationships, premature relationships, and undeveloped relationships. The fear of not finding Mr. or Mrs. Right causes the best of us to jump the gun on relationships that set us back mentally, emotionally, physically, or spiritually. Here is a story that's a prime example:

Pam was consumed with the thoughts of finding her a man in the church. She was so gung-ho about him being in church; she could not see beyond what she wanted. So one day, she met a church-going man. She thought that they would have the perfect relationship, and it turned out to be by far the worst. This man was in the church every time they opened the door; he was in the mass choir and a deacon in the church. He appeared to be a man after God's own heart in the public, but behind closed doors, he was a force to be reckoned with. After Pam had dated him for several months, she noticed that he could not keep a job. She began to look closer at his actions; she found that he would miss work quite often, his mood swings were out of control, and he appeared distant at times. To her amazement, she caught him using drugs when she paid him a surprise visit. Pam was so shocked; she could not believe how he worshiped God like a champ and did drugs like a pauper.

Pam tried to get him into treatment, but he would not go because he had choir practice. She could not understand why choir practice was so important when he really needed help with his drug addiction. The answer came a week later when 2 of the choir members began to fight over him. Pam could not believe that he was cheating, using drugs, and playing with God. She was so angry at herself because God gave her exactly what she asked for. She prayed for a man in church and not for a man that had the church in him. For that reason, she has become very specific about her wants, needs, and desires.

It has become an epidemic; it is so amazing how fear will cause us to settle for inequality to fill the void of loneliness, insecurity, or depression, overriding our instincts or common sense. In order to build a great relationship, we must be willing to become a master at one's likes, desires, and dislikes from the boardroom to the bedroom. We must possess that something that goes above and beyond what's in our bedroom; although, our sexual needs are important; however, it will lose its effectiveness if we do not put the essence of our mind power behind it. If we do not learn the Rules of Relationship and the types of people to avoid when building relationships, we will find ourselves tossed to and fro by the issues of life. For that reason, we must find ways to stimulate the mind, touching the heart, and catering to the inner child from within ourselves as well as within our mate, and the desired people that we come in contact with. If we do not, we are going to lose some brownie points in that area, and trust me; this is an area that we do not want to risk losing in. The competition is fierce, and the moment that we slip up, there is someone waiting to pick-up where we are lacking— married, unmarried, or anything in between. Therefore, it's best that we become consistent in all of our ways and not live by a double-standard, because people are always watching our actions, reactions, and what comes out of our mouth.

2nd Type of Person to Avoid

Avoid People Who Live By A Double Standard

We cannot live by a double standard; we must possess that in which we are looking for. We are all a work in progress; if we don't possess certain qualities right now, we must start working on possessing each one of these characteristics. These qualities may take a little time to manifest and develop, so don't waste time, energy, and money on people, places, and things that contradict what we want and desire. I do not buy into the 50/50 relationship—I buy into the concept of the 100/100 relationship. One must be able to give 100% of himself or herself to make a relationship work; if not, how well do one expect a relationship to work when they are giving half of themselves? Here are a few ideal qualities that we should possess under the 80/20 Rule for ourselves. If one does not possess these qualities, it is not fair to expect them from someone else.

- ☐ Stable.
- ☐ Interdependent.
- ☐ Teachable.
- ☐ Flexible.

- ☐ Respectful.
- ☐ Encouraging.
- ☐ Positive.
- ☐ Loving.
- ☐ Affectionate.
- ☐ Giving.
- ☐ Humorous.
- ☐ Resourceful.
- ☐ Cooperative.
- ☐ Open & Honest.
- ☐ Confident.
- ☐ Wise.
- ☐ Sincere.
- ☐ Supportive.
- ☐ Interesting.
- ☐ Loyal.
- ☐ Resourceful.
- ☐ Unselfish.
- ☐ Not Abusive.
- ☐ Protector.
- ☐ Not Lazy.

When embarking upon our relationship quest, we must make a commitment to patiently persevere through all obstacles regardless of how we feel. Actually, we must consistently think toward greatness by learning how to present ourselves strategically without becoming overbearing or desperate. We must also know and understand our purpose for doing what we are doing, as well as find out what we like and do not like in a relationship. Basically, we need to find out who needs what we have to offer. And, by knowing this, we are then able to create a sense of urgency or hunger for what we are offering. Of course, with experience and perseverance, we are then able to update, enhance, or make our simple plan outstanding by knowing 7 things:

1. Know yourself and your purpose in life.
2. Know how you can make a difference.
3. Know what you want and do not want.
4. Know the impact of what you have to offer.
5. Know your competition.
6. Know how you are going to create the urgency for your qualities.
7. Know how you are going to share what you have to generate positive results in your life.

We must master our qualities by diligently getting to know what's in our heart; while making the adjustments to love, serve, and assist those who we have a relationship with. As the competition challenges us, we must know and understand what we have to offer without becoming insecure and weak about it. We do not have to buy our mate—if a man can be bought with material gain by a woman, he is not worth it, and if a woman can be bought with material gain by a man, she is not worth it. We should never buy love; we must be able to share our love by doing simple things "just because" for our mate, that's within our budget. We must keep our gifts as inexpensive as possible; this will prevent us from losing out before we really begin. Some relationships may work and some may not, so we must keep our budgets to a minimum.

I am not saying that we should not help the person that we are in a relationship with—I am saying that we should not **BUY** the person that we are in a relationship with. It's time out for that Gold-digging mentality.

Weighing the pros and cons of a situation or circumstance are very important when it comes down to risking our integrity in a relationship. Yes, some things may feel good for the moment; but when that moment is over, then what do we do? Is compromising our integrity really worth it? The answer is NO; however, it can teach us a valuable lesson on how important it is to protect ourselves from having a jaded effect on our life. Compromise has often provided temporary comfort to those who want more than what they need. When we allow our conscience to be our guide; eventually, the nudge for correction will come, and it will be left up to us to continue or to refrain.

If you want to stand out, hold steadfast to your integrity and never compromise who God has created you to be or what He has created you to do. People may laugh, talk about you, or even criticize you, but you must not give in to the tricks of the enemy. As a matter of fact, knowing who and what's in your heart will help turn a relentless mind into a productive mind; therefore, taming the thoughts, actions, and reactions regarding those who have zero love for you.

3rd Type of Person to Avoid

Avoid People Who Do Not Love You

The truth about the lack of love could very well be a hard pill to swallow, especially when it cuts really, really deep. Whenever the truth hurts, it's very important that we understand the reasons why. It is imperative that we resolve or control the emotions that are attached to the hurt; otherwise, we will fall victim to our own untruths about ourselves, our situation, our circumstance, or event. If we trust ourselves enough to live a lie, eventually the truth will surface, because it is harder to remember lies that are told in and out of sequence; therefore, making rejection an inevitable consequence of the trust that's broken. In my opinion, lying to buy time is a big time waster, when the truth will yield much better results, or when we can simply plead the 5th. We can't go wrong trusting ourselves with the truth about who we are even if we are rejected.

There are so many things to doubt about life, but God is not one of them. God is Spirit, and He is Truth, and there is no need to doubt that in which we don't understand. Life has a funny way of telling a story that reveals the mystery of its greatness. This relates all too well to someone I know personally, her name is Gracie. Her story actually broke my heart at one point, but God's Master Plan has shown me the bigger picture. Here is the story:

Gracie found herself to be the laughing stock of something that she had no control over. Her mother was a pretty frisky woman who conceived her during a one-night stand. It was nothing more than a rendezvous of pure lust and infatuation that resulted in an unwanted pregnancy. Shawn, Gracie's mother, was not happy about her pregnancy; so she tried everything to terminate the pregnancy, but nothing seemed to work. Although she was very unhappy, she finally accepted the fact that she was going to give birth to another child. One lovely afternoon during Shawn's 8th month of pregnancy, she decides to take a catnap. As she began to rest her head on a pillow, she saw a snake resting calmly on the window-seal beside her bed. Shawn began to scream frantically as she grabbed her belly while gasping for air. Her mother came to see what the commotion was all about, and when she saw the snake, she told Shawn not to touch her belly. Of course, Shawn never mentioned to her mother that she had already grabbed her stomach.

A few weeks later, Shawn goes into labor giving birth to a baby girl named Gracie. Gracie was not a pleasant sight to see; her eyes were wandering in two different directions. She was born cockeyed and licking her tongue like a snake. Shawn was so ashamed that everyone was laughing and making fun of her newborn baby. Gracie was so innocent; she waited patiently, trusting that someone would take care of her, but there she lay in the hospital lonely and ignored. It seemed as if this baby knew that she was unwanted. A few hours later, her grandmother came to visit; she was not surprised that Gracie was born cockeyed and licking her tongue like a snake. She then realized that Shawn did indeed grab her belly when she was frightened by her previous encounter with a snake. Although Gracie was not a pretty sight to see, her grandmother did not care; she loved and adored her without judging or rejecting her.

A few days later before being released from the hospital, the Doctor told Shawn that Gracie may or may not grow out of being cockeyed. She felt as if she could not live with people laughing at her baby, so she *pushed Gracie off on her grandmother. Over the years, after several prayers from her grandmother, Gracie stopped licking her tongue, and her eyes began to straighten on their own. However, she was constantly picked on and laughed at by her family members. They would not allow her to live down the fact that she was born cockeyed and ugly. This little girl became insecure because she could not get away from grown people picking on her and bullying her for no reason.*

Her grandmother felt her pain; she would tell her that she was a beautiful child and that she needed to find her beauty from within. Of course, she did not understand what her grandmother meant, but she held on to the thought of becoming beautiful from within. As a matter of fact, her grandmother taught her to love God first, then love herself, and it would be through her creativity that she would become beautiful enough to love others. Like a little child with a small mind, that was way beyond her comprehension; therefore, her grandmother sent her out to play under a specific oak tree to create something beautiful. Gracie would go to the junk pile next to the oak tree every day to gather her material to create something new and unique. She did this for years, although she played alone, she learned how to build something out of what people rejected. And, this is where Gracie began to find her creativity and beauty.

Although she was very young, she used the principles from her grandmother to spark her journey into greatness. Gracie learned how to question life to learn its valuable lessons and then activating the Law of Reciprocity sharing what she learned with others. She learned that life would open a floodgate of divine wisdom if she shared her lessons, trials, tribulations, failures, and successes while asking life the right questions.

4th Type of Person to Avoid

Avoid People Who Reject You

⌒⌒⌒

We are often taught not to question things; as a matter of fact, we are also taught not to question God, but if we don't ask questions, how will we get the answers? Of course, we are bombarded with the opinions of others; however, there are certain things in life that cannot be answered by anyone else but God. Gracie's grandmother taught her in her language at a young age how to search, plan, and build by the concept of creating something from junk under an oak tree. For her it was fun, she did not realize that she was learning how to strategically build an empire with her grandmother's wisdom. Although Gracie's mother rejected her, it was designed that way—it was her grandmother that was ordained to teach this child the wisdom she needed to become rooted and grounded in her gifting. Now, this is your opportunity to build something beautiful in your life.

Asking the right questions will help us get the tools that we need to build the type of relationships that we desire. Even though Gracie's relationship with her mother was violated at birth, she did not allow it to deprive her of a fulfilled future. Her grandmother taught her how to trust God first, trust herself through her creativity, be kind to everyone, hold on to her integrity, and to trust life no matter what. Gracie is now a drop-dead gorgeous woman with better than 20/20 vision, and she gives love freely with no strings attached. Gracie found that trusting God to be the security blanket over her life, there was nothing that she could not achieve. As compensation for her trust, God gave her beauty for her ashes; and not only that, He granted her a triple portion of love and wisdom that supersedes human comprehension. Although Gracie did make an attempt to buy her mother's love; but, as soon as she could not buy it anymore, her mother rejected her again. That taught Gracie a valuable lesson about buying love—if it's not natural, she does not want it.

I would say rejection is not such a bad thing to become exposed to—once an individual can accept rejection, he or she will become able to overcome obstacles that others would back away from. According to statistics, 80% of success is obtained by 20% of the population, so there are a lot of people who are left behind because rejection has booted them out of that 20% of dreamers and doers. In so many words, 20% of people are willing to do what the other 80% are unwilling or conditioned not to do. Of course, some may not believe in the 80/20 rule, but if rejection is a weakness, it is now time to overcome it to ensure that the fear of failure will not prevent the heart's desire from becoming a reality. Furthermore, from this point forward, if someone rejects us or what we have to offer, simply say "Thank you" and move on. My secret to the 80/20 rule is that we will be rejected by 80% of the people that are not designed to fit into our lives; and, if we do not allow rejection to break us, it then prepares us for the 20% of the positive people, places, and things that will help us to soar into the 80% success category, even with our issues as long as we are not lying to ourselves about our reality. Such as Life! In order to get what you want, there are certain types of people that you are going to have to AVOID.....period.

And, they will avoid you as well. Is that rejection? Absolutely. It's called strategic rejection so to speak. However, this does require a positive attitude.

A positive attitude does not mean that we will not have a negative thought, nor does it mean that we will always do or say the right thing—what it means is that we will positively take responsibility for our actions, reactions, thoughts, or the lack there of. Shifting the blame for what we do, say, or become does not exhibit responsibility, nor does it help us resolve our issues or character flaws. In my opinion, the sooner we own up to what we do, say or become, the sooner we can make the positive adjustments in what has caused us to focus on the negative more than the positive aspects of our relationship; therefore, breaking the victim mentality.

5th Type of Person to Avoid

Avoid People Who Victimize You

We are all sensitive in some way, some more sensitive than others; however, the key is to learn how to deal with our sensitivities. Most often, our sensitivities are usually the result of some sort of pain or trauma, but it only becomes a problem when we allow it to get out of control, or we play the role of being a victim. Playing the victim will get us attention, it will get us what feels like love, or it will get us sympathy; but, it does not bring us wholeness. In my opinion, playing the victim will keep us looking for the next emotional quick-fix that feeds our internal conflict; as a matter of fact, playing the victim role will only allow us enough room to play ourselves in the end, if we do not positively change our mentality about the situation, circumstance or event. This is how Olivia changed her life:

Olivia wasn't brought up in the church, nor did she have an interest in staying in church all day; she felt as if it was overkill. One day, she found a small church that did not have service all day long; so she joined it, hoping that she was doing the right thing. She really became so excited about getting her life right with God; however, a few months later the church gossip started, and the church members began to drag her name through the dirt. She began to get a little discouraged, but she kept going hoping that God would work out some things in her life. She didn't proclaim to be a saint; she knew she had issues, and that's why she was making an attempt to get her life right. Olivia was being victimized in the real world and victimized in the Church as well—she did not know which way to turn. A year later, God did indeed bless her. As a result of her blessing, she blessed the church as well. Not only that, the pastor of this particular church convinced Olivia that God would bless her if she rented a new church building in her name, and she did. She felt as if she did the right thing; but a few months later, they wanted her to pay the rent on the facility every month. Olivia was not that dumb; that was her wake-up call! She lied to the pastor, saying that she could not afford to pay her bills and the bills for the church too. As a result, the church moved out of the building overnight and left her with the rent to pay anyway. Olivia could not believe that she was so naive; she was brainwashed. She was too blind by her blessing to see a wolf in sheep's clothing. A victim again, she weeps…...she cried all night for several days straight; her wounds would not stop bleeding. She did not have a church to run to, so she had to learn how to pray on her own. Olivia did not realize that God would listen to her prayers outside of the church. She did not realize that she had instant access to God; she was really clueless, and she needed help bad. She has everything that one could ask for, she has a big house, she drives a Mercedes, she has money, she is beautiful, she is sexy, she is fine; yet she is down on her knees crying out in pain because she does not know how to effectively pray for herself because she has become a victim again. Everyone is on the take, and she is tired of giving and not receiving. She is tired of being used, she is tired of being victimized, she is just simply tired…after being abandoned and ultimately betrayed by her place of worship. She was willing to do anything to make the pain go away, so she got on her knees praying, asking God to help her overcome this victim mentality.

One day, she was in her office praying; and, a voice spoke clearly to her saying, "You put your faith in the church and not in Me." She immediately stood up yelling, "Oh my God, I am sorry." When she had a problem, she went to the church. When she needed prayer, she went to the church. When she needed healing, she went to the church. When she needed a blessing, she went to the church. She never thought about going to God first before going to the church. She did indeed place her church before God; she worshiped her church, not realizing that she needed to worship God. That moment has changed Olivia's life totally. From that point forward, she reclaimed her life—vowing to go to God first for any and all things. Her spirituality went from 0 to 100; she is not the preachy, preachy type of woman; but, she shoots straight from the hip with love. She does not believe in religion; she believes in a spiritual relationship with the God in Heaven. That is her direct connect, and now she is no longer a victim, because everything happens for a reason in her life; and it's her responsibility to find the lesson to share with the world.

If victimization has caused us to feel lonely, depressed, abandoned, and/or helpless, please seek help—find someone that is trustworthy and talk to them. Now, with that being said, the ultimate goal is to live our lives in victory, while becoming a mentor for the real victims of unfortunate circumstances. Today, start looking for the good in everyone and watch how the natural goodness begins to rise up out of you. Just remember that you were born to love and be loved! So what, if you have been hurt—don't let it take what truly belongs to you, and that is your right to be happy. Be true to yourself, love like you have never been hurt before, and watch how you begin to heal beyond all human understanding—as your well begins to overflow, quenching the thirst of the longing that you have from within as you learn the truth about your circle.

6th Type of Person to Avoid

Avoid People Who Are Selfish

Our life in a relationship is in our ability to give. We cannot be selfish, and the moment that we become selfish, our relationship begins to break down. This is serious. Selfishness is the root cause of ALL divorces! Today, reclaim your integrity—it is your life-line to your peace, prosperity, and sanity. Once that is accomplished, from this point forward, "Do not withhold good from those to whom it is due, when it is in the power of your hands to do so." Proverbs 3:27. If you can help someone, help them. If you can encourage someone, encourage them. If you can love someone, love them. If you can motivate someone, do it. If you can bless someone, bless them with no strings attached. I firmly believe that if for some reason you can't see your way through something, give your way through it—trust me, paying it forward really works. I am living proof. Filling the needs of others can and will open the door to getting our own personal needs, wants, or desires met. When we open our hands first, that enables God to open His hands: As Scripture concurs, "Give, and it will be given to you: good measure, pressed down, shaken together, and running over will be put into your bosom. For with the same measure that you use, it will be measured back to you." Luke 6:38.

Make no mistake about it; caring is the prerequisite for a truly successful life—it is required to love effectively, to give freely or to create anything of value. As it is often overlooked, caring about others builds Godly character from the inside out. Sadly enough, without our ability to care, we will find that we tend to ignore the fact that we have an inner born desire to care about the wants, needs, and the well-being of others. You can easily start caring for others by asking, "How can I help you?" or "What can I do for you?" This will help eliminate the tendency to become selfish. I have found that this is the quickest way to bring down walls with other people as well. This is one **nugget of wisdom** that you will never want to forget—helping others with no strings attached is one of the easiest ways to bring down walls in a relationship and with people. It will also help to keep the walls of SELFISHNESS from forming in your heart. You will thank me later. Trust me on that one!

7th Type of Person to Avoid

Avoid People Who Are Hateful

When people are hateful, mean, or cruel, find yourself an exit quickly. I had to grow up with mean and hateful people, and I made a vow to myself to become a nice person. Hateful people polished me up into the woman that I am today; therefore, I do an about-face when I run into someone who is cruel to innocent people. Even for my family members, if they start getting cruel or hateful around me, I leave....I do not hang around. That is my method of operation—I do not like that type of energy, and I do not make it a secret to anyone. In my opinion, whether you accept or reject the attitude, beliefs, values, actions, or reactions of your parents or family members, there will always be some form of negative influence that must be watched very closely. And, that is why you must be very careful, take it from Daisy:

Daisy was a good ole' country girl from the South, who was conditioned by her parents to accept life without asking questions. She grew up in an extremely negative environment with hateful people and did not know it. She grew up in a hostile environment and did not know it. She grew up in an abusive environment which she did know—she has the scars to prove it. Growing up, Daisy never once heard her mother or father say, I love you to her. Can you imagine never being hugged by your parents? Can you imagine never being kissed by your parents? Can you imagine never receiving affection from your parents? These are some of the things that Daisy could only dream of having. Daisy was tortured by the longing for affection from her parents as she watched her other siblings receive what she could only long for.

One day, Daisy had enough, she was tired of being told that she would never amount to anything, she was tired of her two-faced kinfolks, she was tired of the backbiting, and most of all, she was tired of being beaten for things that she did not do. She slipped into a state of depression as she was beaten to a pulp after refusing to intermingle with her hateful siblings. She felt as if she had nothing else to live for, so she made a decision to end her life. Daisy gave up on herself! She took a whole bottle of her mother's pain medication to make her pain go away. God's hand was indeed on this child; He did not allow her to take her own life, but He made her so sick that she would think twice about doing that again. Daisy vomited to the point where she felt as if she was going to vomit her guts out. As a child she didn't know how to pray; but at that point, she found the words to ask God to take the pain of vomiting away, while vowing never to attempt suicide ever again. The sad thing about this situation is that nobody knew that she took the pills. They did not know because they did not care…how can a child take a whole bottle of prescription pain pills and nobody knows about it? Did her mother not realize that the pills were missing? This child is riddled with pain, vomiting, suffering, and no one does anything. In my opinion, that is child neglect.

When Daisy makes a promise, she's adamant about keeping it. After her vow to God, she took beatings like a champ; her parents thought that something was wrong with her. Daisy learned how to find peace within her very own soul—the most amazing thing about Daisy, she learned how to create the life she wanted mentally, while her body was in a negative situation; therefore, mastering the power of her mind. She also learned how to take herself out of a situation mentally and emotionally while around hateful people, to protect herself physically. With her dedication to herself, she refused to allow anyone to break her willpower to succeed at living her life, or allow anyone to get in her head. As a young child, amazingly, Daisy learned how to change the channel on negativity to focus strategically on the positive. She also knew that when she became an adult, she could choose her attitude, she could choose her values, she could choose her beliefs, she could choose her actions, and she could choose her reactions regardless of her genetic makeup or upbringing. The way she was made to feel as a child, she does not wish that on her worst enemy; therefore, she safeguards herself from the atrocities of hateful people.

As an adult, Daisy has kept her promise to God, and she has kept her promise to herself; and no one believes that this really happened to her because she is a very nice, loving, peaceful, and pleasant person that prides herself on integrity. Daisy takes nothing for granted, and she takes her environment and her relationships seriously. She believes that if God can deliver her from that situation, she must serve and live for Him.

As life would have it, the fruit will never fall far from the tree; therefore, it's going to take discipline and perseverance to overcome or alter a negative DNA structure or mindset to a positive one. One thing you must remember, an undisciplined lifestyle will hinder you from achieving your goals; whereas a disciplined lifestyle will free you to achieve anything your mind can conceive. For that reason, you must become very cautious about what you watch, listen to, read, think about, and the people who you associate with in your inner or outer circle.

8ᵗʰ Type of Person to Avoid

Avoid People Who Are Abusive

We do not deserve to be abused under any circumstance. Find an exit and do not return. The one thing that I have found is that abuse occurs in every culture and at every socioeconomic level. And, regardless of where we are in life, we will think 1 of 4 things:

1. We will think that abuse will never happen to us.
2. We will think that we deserve to be abused.
3. We will think that we do not deserve to be abused.
4. We have the right to abuse.

Most often, we believe that women are more abused than men; however, I beg to differ on that. Men are just as abused as women; they just do not mention it because they are experts at keeping secrets. Actually, men are more susceptible to all forms of abuse except for physical abuse. It is indeed true that more women are prone to physical abuse than men, but with all the other forms of abuse, men rank just as high, if not higher. Of course, men are not going to mention that they are being emotionally abused, mentally abused, economically abused, sexually deprived/manipulated, or being stalked by their wives or girlfriends! Whether it's male or female, abuse is all around us, in our homes, hostile environments in the workplace and in our social endeavors as well. The writing is always on the wall with an abuser or an abusee—so if we can't get away from it, we must learn and understand it to ensure that we do not become the next victim.

The ultimate goal of an abuser is to seek power and precedence over something or someone. The love of power and the fear of losing it will drive an abuser to great extremes. Here are a few things that we need to know:

1. The pains of the past produce our problems of today.

2. The victim as a child often grows up to be victimized as an adult.

3. Abuse victims often become a perfectionist and high achievers.

4. Those who are often abused become abusers.

5. Abuse victims feel they are to blame.

6. Headaches, asthma, body pain, eating disorders are often symptoms of abuse or emotional problems.

7. Abusers are often respected people.

8. Angry people sometimes blame others for their misfortunes.

9. A negative self-image stems from real or perceived deprivation or rejection as well as abuse.

10. Sexual abuse often leads to sexual problems, promiscuity, or secret acts of prostitution.

11. Suppressed emotions often lead to physical symptoms.

12. Forgiveness is essential for emotional healing.

Abuse is unacceptable, regardless of what type it is. Whether we are married, unmarried or anything in between, when there is an itch from within, we will often ask ourselves:

1. What's wrong with me?
2. What have I done so wrong?
3. Why do I keep attracting these types of relationships?
4. Will I ever meet the right person?

Our conditioning or programming from our childhood experiences determine the level of anger we exhibit, our level of self-esteem, as well as our level of security. They amazingly work together regardless of whether we were raised by both parents, neglected by a parent, mistreated by a parent, lost a parent during childhood, abandoned, or whether we had surrogate parents or raised by an institution—positive and negative programming will take place. For the individuals whose parents were physically or emotionally absent, rest assured that there will be self-esteem issues of unworthiness, unlovability, or insecurity that needs to be worked on or worked at on a consistent basis. When dealing with these types of issues, we very well may spend years unlearning, relearning or getting over some things, but we must truly understand the point of origin if we want to really understand who we are as a person, and why we are as an individual.

I have found that negative experiences and hurt produces baggage; and, with every piece of baggage, the unresolved issues get stronger and more frequent. Therefore, we must find a way to refuse the baggage that we do not want to keep, and the best way that I have found is through prayer and avoiding certain types of people. If we develop a deaf ear to who we need to avoid, simply take a look at what Alice has to say about it:

Alice was not accustomed to standing up for herself and what's right; however, she was indeed a very nurturing and caring person who would give you the shirt off her back. She made a choice during her childhood that she would never intentionally make someone feel bad or hurt them in any way. And due to her lack of emotional toughness, she broke like glass. Basically, Alice had a weak backbone that created a sense of desperation for her. She was desperate for love, desperate for a friend, desperate to be seen, desperate to be in control, desperate for attention, desperate to be at the top, desperate, desperate, desperate, and the list goes on. Her desperation stuck out like a sore thumb, so she attracted those who fed off of desperate people. Not only was Alice desperate, but she also used sex as a measurement of love. She felt that she needed to stay with her boyfriend Oscar, and sex him, in order to prove her love. Alice did not feel that a man could really love her without having sex because she never had the opportunity to experience real love. For that reason, she loved him more than God himself.

After being in a relationship with this man for years, Alice denied the fact that cheating had become his middle name. He would lie to her, and she would believe it. She even believed the lies he told her about getting another woman pregnant, until that woman showed up at his place 8 months pregnant. One day, this pregnant woman knocks on the door; and he would not answer it. Every time she knocked, the knock became a little harder and then it went away. A few minutes later, they heard breaking glass; she had thrown a brick in the window to get his attention. Oscar ran outside and tackled this woman like she was a man. Alice frantically watched him beat up this pregnant woman; as he tussled with her, then dragging her in the dirt. The neighbors called the cops to report the incident. Right before the police arrived, he came back in the house and made Alice leave being that she was the only witness to this entire incident. This should have been the writing on the wall for Alice, but she was too naive to see this man for who he really was. As a result of this incident, the pregnant woman that was carrying his baby was hospitalized that night. Sadly, her baby began to die inside of her. Alice had to carry a secret of the real reason why her baby; I mean, their baby died. As a matter of fact, she was afraid to say anything because she did not want to lose Oscar.

A few months later, Oscar found another place and moved Alice in with him. They enjoyed spending time with each other; it was the ultimate relationship that Alice always wanted until he began to push her around. She began to notice that when he became angry, he would become a little violent. It started with a push; she ignored it. Then came the slap, she ignored it. Then came the bloody nose, he apologized for it. Oscar should have become a used car salesman, because he sweet-talked his way out of giving her a black eye and a big bloody lip while convincing her that it was all her fault. Alice felt as if this was her punishment for not saying anything about him beating up his pregnant ex-girlfriend. At this point, she had had enough; she packed her things and went to a battered women's shelter. Alice refused to talk to the counselors about her situation; and not only that, she did not like the living arrangements anyway, so she went back home hoping that things would change.

Oscar promised her that he was going to change and that he was going to seek counseling. He did well for a while, and as soon as he became comfortable within his skin, his anger went through the roof over petty things. By that time, the love that she had once had for Oscar began to fade. Alice had lost all of her trust in him; she was afraid for her life, but she was also afraid to leave him as well. As a result, she began to pray, reading the Bible and asking God to help her. One Saturday morning, Oscar began to argue and push her around. She decided to just walk away from him to prevent any type of unwanted abuse; and, as soon as she began to walk out the door, he grabbed her pulling her down to the floor causing her to fall back on her ankle. Alice screamed as she fell to the floor, she tried getting up, but she could not walk on her right leg. Every time she tried to put her weight on her leg, it felt gritty. She was rushed to the hospital, and they refused to treat her because it appeared to be a sprained ankle, so they sent her to her primary care physician. Alice was in so much pain while they took their precious time to examine her. Once they realized that she had been limping around on a broken leg for almost 6 hours, they immediately took control of the situation rushing her back to the hospital for emergency surgery. Oscar had broken her leg in 2 places, and Alice still lied for him, telling the Doctors that she slipped and fell. Nonetheless, they repaired the damage by putting a plate and screws in her fibula as well as the tibia and then placing a cast on her leg. Her doctor said that she would walk with a limp for the rest of her life, but Alice was not claiming that.

After sitting around the house in physical and emotional pain all day long, she became more determined than ever to get out of that cast and to get out of his house. She started to plan her escape from him; she put her some furniture on lay-a-way and silently started looking for her *a place to live. One day Oscar came home from work early catching her making arrangements to leave him. He started yelling at her, and she politely got up, got her purse while limping out to her car. He ran behind her and dragged her back in the house. All she could think about was when he dragged his pregnant ex through the dirt and how she kept her mouth shut. She began to cry to God like a little baby, because she felt as if she was to blame for him killing his unborn child and now she had to pay the price for her silence.*

As her leg began to heal, so did her heart. God began to strengthen her to walk away from this man and to never return. In the wee hours of the morning, Alice was awakened out of a dead sleep, and a voice said to her, "GO NOW." She felt puzzled and a little delusional; the voice spoke again saying, "GO NOW." She then recognized that it was the Voice of God, giving her the signal to run for her life. And she ran! She got an apartment, while enjoying living on her own. A few months later, Oscar found her. He knocked on the door, and her biggest mistake was letting him in. He falsely accused her of taking his movies, and she got so upset that she yelled at him. He then hits her so hard that she literally saw stars. When she regained consciousness, her face felt a little deformed—so she went to look in the mirror, and her face was twisted. He broke her jaw, knocking it out of the socket. He knew that he would be arrested, and his career would go down the drain; therefore, he made a powerful threat to kill her if she told anyone. Alice knew that he meant it, because she saw how he arrested innocent people, she saw how he trumped up charges on drug dealers, she saw how he used his badge to manipulate people, she knew his dirty hidden secrets, and he knew that she held the key to his demise; but, she loved her life a little more. So again, she covered for him. She lied to the doctors; she lied to her parents; she lied to people, and most of all, she lied to herself.

As a great disappointment, her face required extensive

reconstructive surgery—after they finished putting all kinds of screws and plates in her face, they wired her mouth shut; which gave her the perfect alibi to plead the 5th. Despite whether she said anything or not, her anger was boiling over, and she had to find a way to get back at him. After many months of thinking and pondering, she had the perfect plan. She knew that he hated drug dealers, and she knew which one of the drug dealers he hated the most. As a result, she began to date Pablo, one of the biggest drug dealers in town.

Alice could not have had a better plan; because this was indeed a low blow to Oscar's ego as he became the laughing stock on the force. Alice used this relationship as a way of getting revenge, but after her newness had wore out, Pablo began to use, abuse, mistreat, and cheat on her continuously; therefore, causing her plan to backfire. She felt that she had to deal with it because she did not want to start over with another failed relationship. Alice knew that what he was doing to her was wrong, but she accepted it because she felt as if she was bought, stamped, and paid for! As time went on, he engaged in multiple relationships and rejected her because he knew she was not going anywhere. This was a very hard time for her mentally, physically, emotionally, and spiritually because all she wanted was to be loved by someone or just anyone. She felt as if she stepped out of the pot and into the frying pan. After many physical attacks from this man, she was paralyzed with fear of hitting him back. He got so carried away with abusing Alice that one night he slapped her out of her chair onto the floor and started kicking her. There she lay on the kitchen floor in the fetal position, shocked, crying and in pain. Once again, she hears a voice speaking to her. He said, "Get up, if you don't stand up for yourself, people will kick you around for the rest of your life."

Alice immediately stood up, girded up her loins, wiped her tears away and said to Pablo, "Don't you ever put your hands on me ever again; if you do, one of us are going to jail, and one of us are going to *hell." Alice spoke those words with courage and authority that came from God himself. It frightened Pablo so bad that he refused to ever put his hands on Alice again.*

From that day forward, Alice put her trust in God. Alice did move on, and God granted her the ability to put abusive relationships behind her to ensure that she's able to deal with the real issues of her past. She found out the hard way that unrestrained emotions and feelings can spark a desire to do something very unwise; therefore, making it imperative to think through what she's doing and the reasons why. This will help you to make wise decisions even when you are going through a very challenging situation or circumstance. For Alice, before she enters into any relationship, she always asks herself, "What is it going to cost me?" If the cost is too high, she moves on with pride to make sure that the relationship is equally yoked to ensure that her circle stays intact.

CHAPTER 2

Your Roaring Circle

With God all things are possible; however, when we are learning, preparing, or positioning ourselves to embark upon our dream, we must open up ourselves to learn from others who are doing what we desire or who are going in the same direction of our desires. There is a learning process that goes with dream building that cannot be overlooked; it's imperative that we become interdependent to ensure that we are availing ourselves to inter-development. That means that we are able to work together with others as a team to develop ourselves to the next level of our creativity.

It is often said that we become who we hang around with, which I have found that statement to be very true. We have an inner circle and outer circle of relationships; and, we must understand the difference between the two. If not, we will have a constant flow of people in and out of our lives providing little or no substance to the building of our Empire from within. Everyone has a role to play in our lives whether we like it or not; therefore, we must learn how to create an inner circle where we allow people close to our heart; and, an outer circle where they are not in our heart—they are at arm's length so to speak.

How do we build our circle without losing ourselves in the midst of change? The first step to building our circle is to understand that we are not able to control everything. We cannot control others, nor should we violate their will—if we have not noticed by now, even God will not violate our will. There is no need to keep up with the Joneses! They moved out of the neighborhood a long time ago! If one has not noticed by now, God gives us options by allowing the issues of life to consume us; but the bottom line, we make our own choices. In my opinion, that is where gaining control over our lives begin—it is indeed with our choices. However, the moment that we think that we need to fix someone else, that is the moment that we need to take a look from within to fix self. We are not here to fix people; we are here to help, motivate, and encourage others—fixing people is God's job, not ours because we are all imperfect in some area of our lives. We as a people must recognize that we are a source of inspiration to someone, and it is through that disappointment that we unwaringly lead those who look up to us astray. Nevertheless, it is our responsibility as a child of the Most High to lead without intentionally causing dismay to those who are counting on us to lead them.

Every generation must become better than the previous one, and if we are digressing in that formality, we must gain control over our lives to leave a legacy worth leaving behind. Our inner circle is our LEGACY. Our outer circle should become a source of empowerment or inspiration inwardly and outwardly. If it's not doing that, that's justification for reevaluation on someone that may need to be avoided. In my opinion, as we mature, if our circle does not change, then something is wrong. Change is a part of the Cycle of Life, and if we have not expanded our circle—it's too **SMALL**. We have not gone through all of our challenges for nothing; we have not overcome insurmountable defeat to allow it to go in vain—it is time to gird up our loins, get back on track, and live the life that God has predestined for us to live. Everything we need is already within us, every experience has provided a roadmap for us to follow, and all we need to do is become a master over our mind, instincts, emotions, and the divine wisdom from within. Although we may not be able to explain a lot of things about our lives, what's taking place, or the reasons why; but if we can embrace or open ourselves up to the Wisdom of God, I promise that He will redefine everything about our mind, our emotions, and our instincts; therefore, giving us the ability to move into our faith and favor at the appropriate time. Let me say this, faith and favor without God will render one's mind scattered, emotions all over the place, and our instincts ineffective. In my opinion, if that is what's happening, it is better to use the tool that God has given us to gain our POWER back, and that is the power of PRAYER.

9th Type of Person to Avoid

Avoid People Who Judge You or Put You Down

There are people who are out there that get an adrenaline rush by intentionally hurting others; and, if that's the case—I need you to RUN from this individual. This type of person will create bad blood between the two of you, and more than likely, they have a lot of enemies anyway. Find an exit quickly because this is an emotionally and mentally abusive individual. Karma is a stickler regarding our hypocritical behavior, especially when we judge others for the same things that we are guilty of or when we judge others to put them down. The moment that we become big headed or arrogant about being perfect, our conscience will give us a mental flashback as a warning to correct our behavior. If it is not corrected Karma will knock a few notches off our belt; and if still left uncorrected, the issues of life will bring us down to reality exposing all of our skeletons. Please do not allow your skeletons, your weaknesses, or hang-ups to cause you to fall by the wayside because of a deaf ear to wisdom, a desire to make others feel bad, or to simply pick on them. Here is a story that touched me:

As a child, Tina suffered from a reading disorder—she would read words that were not there and her comprehension skills were extremely poor. If that wasn't enough, she had a stutter as well. She was able to hide her flaws most of the time by staying silent; but, when she did speak, she stumbled over her words. This little child was already afraid of people, and now she has to deal with her classmates laughing at her, picking on her, and judging her because she could not articulate words very well. Although, she was a very smart little girl; her flaws made her feel inferior to those who appeared not to have any flaws at all. As a result, Tina shut down when she was around people; it was hard to get her to communicate. One would think that this child was illiterate, but she was so far from that; she was an Honor Roll Student that graduated in the top 10% of her class. I was puzzled by this little girl; but she said that if she opened her mouth people would not think she was smart, so she would rather just "BE SMART" instead. She said that she was not going to allow another child to stop her from getting her education, because she was tired of having to go to work after school and on the weekends picking oranges in the hot sun, then coming home dirty and stink. That was enough embarrassment for her, and she did not want to deal with anyone who did not understand her situation. She never had a day off—she did not have the luxury of playing like a normal child; and, the only way that God could change her life was through her ability to learn. Therefore, there was no need to talk or respond to anyone that was not smarter than her or helping her with her situation.

As time progressed, she learned how to respect her flaws while developing the discipline to become better. Her first step of discipline came when she started reading the Bible every day. As she read the Bible aloud, she would ask God to polish up her reading and comprehension skills. She did not become an expert reader overnight, but her discipline paid off quite well. She is now a speed reader with excellent comprehension skills that's a step above the rest. Oh, by the way, she no longer has a stutter. She prayed her stutter away—she would recite, "My tongue is a pen of a ready writer" over and over until her stutter ceased. Today, this woman is so well-spoken; it's unbelievable how her respect and discipline enabled her to top the charts with her written and spoken words of wisdom.

The twist to the story was that she did not have a reading disorder; it was a gift! This child's mind was auto-correcting the words that should have been there—she was correcting mistakes as a child without realizing what she was doing. She was reading material like she would have written it, and by the teacher yelling at her made her nervous. Once Tina learned what she was doing, she was better able to correct it. Tina also learned that impediments are designed to drive greatness out of us regardless of how it may seem at the time. As she looked back at the classmates who picked on her, now she realizes that it was only a distraction to keep her from learning as it was indeed her blessing in disguise.

An impediment is basically an obstruction or hindrance that will create a superficial image of weakness. When a weakness is exposed to others, most often, we retreat out of shame instead of taking our weakness and turning it into something great. A weakness exposed is better than a weakness covered up. As a matter of fact, an exposed weakness will give us more of an incentive to work on that area; but on the other hand, when our weakness is covered up, it is easier to overlook or make excuses for it. The truth is that we all have some form of impediment. Some are able to cover them up better than others, but in all reality, we all fall short in some area of our lives. This is not the time to worry about falling short or being perfect! Just remember, an impediment cannot keep you blocked if you look for the benefit. When you do that, greatness is inevitable creating an open door of opportunity for you to take advantage of. The internal and external pressures of a flawed weakness gave Tina a reason to take one day at a time.

To truly embrace the power of our circle, we must understand that no one is absolutely perfect, we are born into a World of Sin, and we are all subject to human nature. If we look around us, we will see that we will never have to train a child to do wrong—they will naturally do the wrong thing for "Foolishness is bound up in the heart of a child." Proverbs 22:15; yet, it is our responsibility to teach them to do right! This same concept applies to our attitude—our mind will naturally gravitate to the negative until we train it to look automatically for the positive.

10th Type of Person to Avoid

Avoid People That Violate Your Conscience

If people are chirping in your ear about wrong doings, walk away. If people are pressuring you to violate your conscience, walk away. If people are pressuring you for your secrets, walk away—as long as you know and understand the truth about you, does not mean that you have to tell the whole world unless it's positive. If it's negative or condemning, put it away; and if you cannot bury it, then keep your innermost secrets or your most incriminating skeletons to yourself. You really don't know who is or who is not envious of who you are, what you do, or what you may become; and, if they feel threatened in any way, they may use your past against you as leverage.

When we begin to rebel against life, we will find that life will begin to expose the people, places and things that contribute to our condition. Once we know what pushes our button or violates our integrity, we must stay away from it;

and, if we are not able to stay away, limit contact or exposure to it. My philosophy is to keep it simple and stop allowing people to chat in our ears before we have a talk with God about whatever it is. If we find ourselves hurt about something or someone, when speaking with God, we must evaluate the three sides of the story: our side, their side, and the truth. By doing so, it allows us to understand our role in the situation, circumstance, or event, it allows us to forgive, it allows us to take our power back, and it allows us to move on as if we have never been hurt before. If you allow your conscience to become your guide, I guarantee that this will keep integrity on your side while keeping the silent enemy from within at peace. As a rule of thumb, play your cards close to your chest, because God has allowed certain things to happen to you for your growth and not your demise; and I must say that it's hard to embrace the fullness of life when you are allowing the skeletons of your past to create a thicket of your old mindset. Let it go—you knew it wasn't going to work anyway! From this point on, stay away from relationships that violate your conscience, period! Save yourself the hurt, emotional turmoil, and shame.

Why do we always want what we don't have? I must say that it is human nature—we are born with the desire for more. This could very well be a good thing, or it could very well be a bad thing, depending upon the intent of our heart. The intent of the heart will determine whether our desire for more is just or unjust. Of course, we all have our likes and dislikes, but when we are not sure of them, we will tend to follow the likes and dislikes of others that feed into the discontentment of what we already have. Our freedom of choice is the one reason why we do what we do, say what we say, and want what we want; however, the key is to become a good steward over what we have first, and then set goals to attain more. For example, if we want a better job, we must exude the Spirit of Excellence in the job that we already have. If we want a better car, we must take care of the one we have. If we have a desire for a new relationship, we must make sure that we did not mistreat anyone in our previous relationship. If we want to lose weight, we must be happy with ourselves at our present weight while developing a healthy mental attitude. As the list goes on, we must master our present state of being before setting our minds on other things, because wanting people, places, and things for the wrong reason will do us a great disservice. Most of the time we will not miss what we have lost until it's gone; besides, most of our blessings are right under our nose, but we are too blind to see it because of our human nature. It is imperative that we make sure that we become a good steward over what we have to ensure that we want people, places and things for the right reason.

When creating your inner and outer circle of relationships, all you have to do is stop trying to overcomplicate life, learn to live in peace, pray about everything, and embrace the Wisdom of God to govern your mind, your emotions, and your instincts. Once this is done, I promise you that the Mind, Body, Soul, and Spirit will make a true believer out of you, changing your whole outlook on life!

11th Type of Person to Avoid

Avoid People That Are Phony

We have to learn how to become true to who we are. In building a successful relationship, we must be able to discuss our likes, dislikes, fears, frustrations, and expectations of each other to ensure that there will not be any surprises later on. In the midst of doing so, we must never lose our personal identity for a relationship. If we have to lose our identity for a person, then they may not be the one for us. Living up to someone's expectations of us becomes hard when we are not naturally that way; because in due time, that face will come off.

The power of a first impression could be misleading based upon our differences in beliefs, style, thinking, etc., causing us to lose out on something or someone that we may have misunderstood. Appearance does reveal a lot, but there are certain things that it will not reveal until an understanding is developed. Some people make an investment in their outside appearance; some people make an investment in their inside appearance, some invest in both, and some could care less about either. Regardless of how our investment is made, everyone is rich in some way, shape, or form—some are rich in health, some in love, some in money, some in ideas, etc. Never underestimate a person because of their occupation, what they drive, what they are wearing, where they live, etc. Furthermore, you will never know the true value of something until you examine its contents. So, in order to release untapped potential, treat everyone like a million dollars and watch how your circle of successful relationships becomes whole.

The true essence of our strength lies in our ability to use our mind to better govern our attitude, actions, and reactions. In my opinion, it does not matter to me what type of show a person puts on in front of me, what they wear, what they drive, how much money they have in their pocket—I pay attention to how they treat the people that they do not need. That tells me everything that I need to know about that person; and, it also tells me whether or not I need to AVOID them. One thing that I have learned in building relationships is that safeguarding our mind is a full-time job! As we all know, we are a constant work in progress, and we cannot afford to become too comfortable with people, places and things that pull us in a direction that we are not compelled to go. When we allow ourselves to be led in the wrong or unwise direction, we will soon find ourselves ineffective in that particular area. In today's time, with the fast movement of social media, we can become known for what we want to be known for; however, once our integrity is lost through telling lies, it is hard to regain. "Lying lips are an abomination to the Lord, but those who deal truthfully are His delight." Proverbs 12:22. We have learned in a previous chapter that a good name is chosen; and, what we do not realize is that our integrity, credibility, and character are a part of who we are. Who cares about a name, integrity or credibility as long as we are getting what we want, right? Wrong, whether we are at the top or the bottom of the ladder of success, we need to exercise caution when our integrity is involved, because we may not be able to undo something once it is done.

12th Type of Person to Avoid

Avoid People That Kick You When You Are Down

Our daily regime opens the floodgate of what tomorrow is going to bring. As we mold and shape our destiny to build good solid relationships, we cannot forget about the impact of what we are doing right now. Of course, we all have hope for tomorrow; but our tomorrow has the hope of what we are doing today in order to set in motion its very own agenda. If for some reason we fall short, we don't need people in our lives to kick us when we are down—if they do....leave them alone. Our setbacks are basically our setup for a real blessing, if we do not give up on ourselves. I firmly believe in leaving no stone unturned, and I ran into someone else who thinks the same way:

Lisa was considered to be a profound risk taker; as a result, she found herself living on the edge dealing with a lot of failures. Of course, with each endeavor, her risk became a little higher until she fell flat on her face losing everything. The friends that she thought she had, did not call nor did they check on her. Lisa was totally abandoned by everyone, including her family. She became the talk of the town—it seemed as if everyone was waiting for the opportunity to laugh and talk about her. In Lisa's moment of loneliness, she began to question her purpose in life. What she found out about herself was astounding. As a result of her failure, she realized that she was a people pleaser. She allowed herself to become driven by the opinions and the influences of her friends; therefore, clouding her judgment regarding what she was really supposed to be doing. As a result, Lisa became very strategic in her thoughts, actions, reactions, and most of all, her time. She began to manage her time like it was a full-time job—she turned off the television and the radio, so that she could listen to her thoughts and the lack thereof. After several months of listening to life and asking questions, she began to receive dynamic answers. She realizes that her input, determined her output, and if she was not putting out the right things, she changed her thoughts. Lisa took one block of her life and began to build an empire. Although it did not happen overnight, she continued to build her life as if she had a systematic plan. She discovered that if you find the "what" in life the "how-to" develops. When she sets a goal for herself, she asks herself the who's, what's, when's, where's, how's and why's of life. She firmly believes that your effectiveness is increased when you know what you want, and why you want it. Of course, no one likes to be wrong; and, self-correction can become difficult at times. However, when we do not know or understand the reason behind our ineffectiveness we become resistant to change, especially when our back is up against the wall.

It was through the bumps and bruises that Lisa gained her strength, wisdom, and know-how. Lisa built an Empire that blew my mind—I could not believe what she builds in the midst of what people considered her downfall. This woman secretly built an EMPIRE while people laughed, talked, ridiculed, mistreated, and ignored her; and the most amazing thing about it—she did not try to defend herself. When they realize what she had accomplished, it was too late—the damage was already done. They were already on the AVOID list.

If you ever find yourself on the wrong road or at a dead end; quickly, re-evaluate the situation, find out where you went wrong and simply, turn around. Falling down is inevitable! It's going to happen; THAT'S LIFE! If life knocks you down, GET BACK UP AGAIN!

13th Type of Person to Avoid

Avoid People That Pry

Why do people violate the privacy of others? There are many different reasons why our privacy could be violated; however, I will discuss a few. The most obvious on behalf of the violator will be due to insecurity, lack of trust, or suspicion; but, before I go any further, I must say that any parent that has a child under the age of 18 living at home must understand that their child has no privacy. We are held accountable for our children, and it's imperative that we know them from the inside out. If we do not know our child's favorite color, their likes/dislikes, what motivates them, what discourages them, their dreams, their goals, what hurts them, or what they truly want to become when they grow up, then we are giving them too much privacy. Now, if we violate the privacy of those who are not our children, we are out of order!

Who wants a snooping partner in a relationship? This is one of the quickest ways to sabotage a relationship. Violating

Chapter 2 | Ruby Fleurcius

someone's privacy is a BIG no-no. You do not have to follow someone, go through their phone, or go through their emails, especially when you need to focus on building a relationship and not tearing it down. And, if you feel as if you have to do that—you do not need to be in a relationship with that person anyway. That is TOXIC…..Why would you want to torture yourself that way? You have too much time on your hands to babysit a grown person.

The moment a person thinks about violating the privacy of someone else or violating the will of someone that is not their child, are all signs of insecurity! If that type of behavior is not dealt with properly, it will bring about a form of self-demise or outright compromise. In my opinion, if a person has enough time to pry into the lives of others, that's less time being spent on SELF and taking care of their family responsibilities. Furthermore, that is definitely out of order according to SCRIPTURE; therefore, we will bring the sword to our own house, then we will wonder what's wrong. If one would focus that same amount of energy on becoming a better person by loving, sharing, and caring—we will not have time to look for dirt on others, especially when we have a little dirt ourselves.

If we are not getting paid to investigate, snoop, or pry into the lives of others, we should exercise extreme caution when doing so. Snooping, prying, or following someone violates trust, and violated trust creates undue tension in a relationship as well as undue emotional turmoil. What you need to know will come to you; you don't have to break the law or put yourself or your family in jeopardy to get it! In my opinion, this is the first subtle sign of a control freak.

So stay focused on your own life, and if you are wasting time trying to get the 411 on someone other than self and family—stop it! In my opinion, the same drive that nudges an individual to try to get the 411 on or about someone will be the same information that could possibly lead to us making that 911 call to undue the chaos or confusion that we may have brought to our own house.

When we look for dirt on someone to eventually throw mud, we will find that the residue of mudslinging will always leave its mark on our hands. Look for the good in others in all that you do, regardless of how it may appear, while exercising the value of respected space.

14th Type of Person to Avoid

Avoid People That Are Control Freaks

When we feel like a prisoner in a relationship, we will look for ways to escape; if not physically, but definitely mentally and emotionally. We must experience a sense of freedom in a relationship in order for it to work properly. We must always let them know that they have options and that we value their wants and needs. This is a part of our priority in a relationship. As a word of caution, the control freak's victim may allow them to think that they are in control, but bossing a grown person around will cause them to silently seek their freedom elsewhere.

How can we spot a control freak? There are times when it's obvious to spot a control freak, especially when they are trying to control, manipulate, and bribe others to do what they want to be done. However, there are silent control freaks that are not so obvious with his or her behavior, because they have learned how to conceal their behavior to get what they want, like a wolf in sheep's clothing. Now, the question is, "How can we spot a wolf in sheep's clothing?" In order to spot this type of individual, one must open up their eye gates, ear gates, and instincts; and, if we are emotional, we may miss their cue! One must get out of his or her feelings, if they do not have a desire to become the next victim—exuding too many emotions when dealing with a control freak or a wolf in sheep's clothing, clouds our sense of judgment, while clueing them in on our weaknesses or our pressure points. In my opinion, there are a few signs that I look for to truly understand who or what I am dealing with— the first sign is out of control anger problems. It does not matter if they are nice to us right now, when this person does not get what they want or cannot control the situation, their niceness to us will be out the window, and we will see them for who they really are; hopefully by that time, it's not too late. The second sign, we must pay attention to how they are treating other people, because the same way that they treat others will be the same way that they will treat us when we get their timing wrong. The third sign, if this person is abusive verbally, mentally, physically, emotionally, or spiritually—BEWARE. These are tell-tale signs that this individual may have a problem with respecting others and that they may lack a conscience; therefore, it is imperative that one must tread with caution. If not, expect to become the next victim, because a control freak or the wolf in sheep's clothing is truly a victim who is recruiting or creating other victims to keep the cycle of human trauma, hurt, and destruction going to contribute to the mental and emotional anguish. If you are the control freak or the wolf in sheep's clothing, there is hope for you. You have an opportunity to replace your negative characteristics with positive ones such as love, joy, peace, kindness, goodness, faithfulness, gentleness, and self-control. Remember, a good name is chosen—choose to do the right thing, and watch how God send blessings your way when you least expect it, regardless of what anyone thinks of you or says about you; just don't get caught with your pants down.

15th Type of Person to Avoid

Avoid People That Are Ungrateful

Ungratefulness, or that nothing is ever good enough attitude is the type of attitude that will keep our blessings eluding us every time we turn around. As a matter of fact, if we see ourselves taking one step forward and two steps back that are an indication that we must check our level of gratefulness. We need to check whether we are going in the wrong direction, whether we involve ourselves in the wrong things, or whether we are hanging around the wrong people, etc. And, once we turn our ungratefulness into an ongoing state of appreciation, we will find that our lives will do an about-face, and our conscience will begin to open up in ways that would not open otherwise.

When we allow our conscience to become our guide, we will find that our conscience will not miss a beat—our conscience will free us, and it will ultimately convict us when needed. Although our conscience can be sifted based upon our environment, conditioning or the lack thereof; however, we all know the difference between right and wrong, good and bad, as well as the positive and the negative, even if we pretend as if we do not know the difference.

16th Type of Person to Avoid

Avoid People That Do Not Have A Conscience

If we run into someone who appears not to have a conscience, RUN—there is a problem from within! "A prudent man sees evil and hides himself, the naive proceed and pay the penalty." Proverbs 27:12. Hurting innocent people is greatly frowned upon, and the Law of Karma is in high effect, so be careful around this individual….. If our conscience doesn't convict us of our wrongdoings, misbehavior, betrayals, or deception, we will find that the ones closest to us will begin to lose trust in us, or we will begin to accuse others of the same things that we are secretly guilty of. Believe it or not, our conscience and the conscience of others will reveal our true character through our actions, our reactions, our responses, and our spoken words. For me, I consider the conscience to be the "Writing on the Wall" of what's to come—all we need to do is take the time to read what it is saying, and not change it based on how we are feeling, what we want it to say, or who we have a desire to be in a relationship with. Here is a story that opened my eyes:

Silvia fell in love with a man that was not in love with her; he was only in love with her mental capabilities. He saw an opportunity to use her knowledge to build his dream. Even though she knew he was infatuated with her intelligence, she knew that she could make him love her by having sex with him and cover up the fact that he could not read or write well. Of course, she did win temporarily; but as time progressed in the relationship, she started selling her soul to him to fill a lonely void. Yes, a lonely void that was buried deep within her heart; or better yet, a void that was created to avoid the calling that God had on her life. She was ashamed of God, and she was ashamed of the gifts that He had placed in her; therefore, squandering her blessings with someone who could care less about God or what he wanted Silvia to do. How can one be ashamed of God? How can one be ashamed of the gifts from within? Nevertheless, she was ashamed to be associated with God.

Every morning this little red bird would come to the window and pecked on it as if he was trying to say something; therefore, creating a sincere tugging in Silvia's heart. She knew that God had a calling on her life, but she did not want to give up this man. She knew that he was a bad influence on her; she knew that she needed to make a decision, but she could not resist the temptation of living the fast lifestyle. Until one day during a thunderstorm, lightning pierce through that same window the little red bird pecked on, hitting Silvia in the back of her leg. Her leg felt as if it was on fire, as it began to shake out of control. There she lay on the floor praying, while Nick, the man she claims to love, laughed hysterically. He did not call for medical help; he gave her a pill to sleep it off, and left the house because he had plans. Although she survived being struck by lightning, the thought of Nick laughing and by him not taking her to the hospital, did indeed shift her heart away from him. What type of person would laugh at someone being struck by lightning? That should have been her sign to walk away from him, but she was still blind.

Although the little red bird continued to peck on the window daily, as she developed a deaf ear to God's will and His way. Her shame of devoting her life to God had somehow clouded her sense of judgment. One night she was invited to a birthday party, she decided that it was worth spending time with her so-called friends. As soon as she and Nick pulled up to the club, she heard a voice saying, "This is your last night." She played it off saying, "Okay, this is my last time going to a club." Throughout the whole night, she kept on hearing, "This is your last night, this is your last night." As a result, she became very uncomfortable, deciding to leave the club early. Of course, she did not express her concerns to Nick; she just pretended as if she was getting sleepy. For some reason, the late night hunger pains began to kick-in, so they made a pit stop at the Waffle House. While there, they began to crack jokes about the 2 officers in the restaurant eating waffles instead of donuts. As they left the restaurant, they still chuckled at the officers.

As soon as they arrived home, when they walked in the house something appeared unusual. Silvia just blew it off, but Nick took it seriously. He noticed that things were out of place, so he secretly grabbed his gun to ensure that Silvia did not panic. As soon as she walked into the bedroom with their take-out in hand, shots began to ring out. Silvia gets shot, she then yells, "MY GOD." At that moment, everything *from that point on went in slow motion—her life flashed before her in a fraction of a second. All of her dreams, all of her goals, everything that she would ever do in life were placed before her at that moment. As she walked through the tunnel leading up to the light, she stopped, turned around and said, "I am not finished. I can't leave yet." As soon as she made that statement, a presence beyond human understanding covered her. She began to feel her life coming back as she slumps down in a corner like a little rag doll. After the shooting had ceased, they could hear that help was coming. The 1st officers on the scene were the same 2 officers that they laughed at, a few minutes earlier at the Waffle House. They are grateful that those 2 officers chose waffles instead of donuts that night. Nick was shot as well, he and Silvia survived; but one of the burglars was not so lucky. The media was all over the place; there were so many different stories about what happened, some lies, some truths, and half-truths alike. Silvia was ashamed of living for God; now the media really made her shame worth serving God. The media cause Silvia to lose her job, lose her friends, and lose her privacy. They camped out on her doorstep; actually, they made her life a living hell until she was glad to serve God.*

After the investigation, the burglar turned out to be a friend of the guy that threw that spur-of-the-moment party, which happens to be Silvia's sister's boyfriend's friend, if that makes any type of sense. To add insult to injury, it was also the boyfriend of one of the women that Silvia's boyfriend was sleeping with. The botched up burglary was set up to teach Nick a lesson about sleeping with another man's woman; however, they did not expect Nick and Silvia to return home early. You are talking about a party without a conscience! Everything had gotten all twisted up over a woman, which almost cost Silvia, who knew nothing about this until after the fact, her life.

Thank God, that situation made her choose to serve God

with no shame attached to it. Silva says that moment has changed her life forever, because there was a spiritual covering that was beyond human covering and protecting her from bullets that were flying right by her head. She had to live those few minutes, and it has changed her spiritual life forever.

Take nothing for granted…avoid people that do not have a conscience and you know who they are….it does not take a rocket scientist to figure that out.

17th Type of Person to Avoid

Avoid People Who Steal From You

Whatever we do in life, there will be a little give and take, ups and downs, positives and negatives, or setups and setbacks; but, this is where we must become very careful about the relationships that we entertain. If we entertain a relationship that takes more than we are willing to give, then we will get caught up on the losing end of the deal. I speak all too well from experience. I entertained a relationship that I wasn't too particularly interested in; but, to kill time—I entertained it anyway. When he found out that I wasn't serious about the relationship, he broke into my house and robbed me of everything I had of value. He shut my business down completely; I did not have any computers, all of my manuscripts were gone, printers, business contacts, documents, connections, flash drives, etc. I cried like a little baby….the Empire that it took 10 years to build was torn down overnight for the lack of love and his insecurities. He had hoped that I would lose everything and come running to him to build his business instead; but, I refused. That was an insult to me. A man steals my equipment, shutting my business down, so that I can build his business on the sly to lock me down, the devil is a lie…..

No matter what this man did to try to make me love him—it never worked. My Empire is connected to my heart; if a person messes with my business, they mess with my heart—that's how I build the lives of others. That is my secret door to wisdom and inner healing for me, which is my lifeline. When a man crosses that line, he is cut off, period. No questions asked. Although, I had to play his game for a minute to get myself together; but, I put my trust in God to restore that in which the cankerworm had stolen, and He did. I am here to write this story today, and it has indeed made me a better woman to truly understand what types of people to avoid.

We are not designed to stay in one place and if we are comfortable with what we are doing that means that growth is not taking place in our lives. Wherever there is a lack of growth, we will find that we will naturally become a sluggard in that particular area if left unchecked; therefore, creating a comfort zone attracting the people, places, and things that contribute to that zone of choice.

CHAPTER 3

The Don't Get Caught Roar!

There are many other do's and don'ts in the Bible regarding our character, our attitude, the way in which we communicate, and the way we treat others. However, my goal is to bring them to life to ensure that we are able to apply them to today's ratchetness that's taking place all around us.

Have you ever had an overwhelming desire for something that was strictly forbidden? Did the desire consume your every thought? Did it drive you insane not to have it? When we talk about the forbidden fruit, Adam & Eve will often come to mind. However, since the fall of Adam and Eve, we've had to battle against the sweet temptation of what's forbidden. Of course, we often like to blame Adam & Eve for our short-comings. However, they cannot assume responsibility for that in which we are willfully able to choose. As you very well know, promiscuity is everywhere—in our churches, in our schools, on the job, and in our very own homes. A lot can be determined about a person's character, values, and standards by their sexual wants and desires.   Therefore, if we do not want to get caught up, we must become totally aware of what types of people that we need to avoid.

18th Type of Person to Avoid

Avoid People That Are Arrogant

Sex is not bad, but the way we use it could be bad for us, or the misuse of it could become even more devastating, especially when we are cheating. Affairs may be exciting at first; but, when we partake of a forbidden fruit, the flame will start to take a little more energy and time.   For example, we will start staying out a little longer, we may start going to work a little later, we may take longer lunches, etc.   All of which may have an impact on our performance, our finances, or our reputation with our family. When we use sex as a weapon or tool, we will begin to listen to negative outside influences, and we will find that our decisions become swayed by those who tell us what we want to hear.   When we allow temptation to consume our mind, our body will soon follow. This is how the cycle of lust ignites the burning desire to have that in which is strictly forbidden. As a matter of fact, we often partake of the forbidden for several reasons:

- Power.
- Money.
- Sex.
- Curiosity.
- Appearance.
- Challenge.
- Ego Boost.
- Fun.
- Lack.
- Pain.
- Companionship.
- Loneliness.
- Greed.
- Fear.
- Anger.

Some measure their status by how many sexual partners they have, how many relationships they can obtain, or how many people that they can deceive. They change partners like they change shoes, and they may say that it does not have an effect on them because it is fun, but I must say that it does have an effect. The effects may come later in a person's life in many shapes and forms. As a matter of fact, committing adultery and being addicted to sex or relationships are not any different from being addicted to drugs, smoking, food, or alcohol—they will all destroy your life!

Sex is portrayed on television as if everybody should be doing it, but the effects it will have mentally, physically, emotionally, and spiritually are not mentioned. Sexual looseness is devastating to all involved. Sex is more than just a physical issue, and toying around with it will get a person burned in more ways than one. Some of you say, "I can do anything I want to." And, you are right, but everything that looks good is not always good.

Sex is not to be used as a weapon or a trap, or it will lead to low self-esteem, self-hate, emptiness, confusion, frustration, or darkness in a relationship. Some use sex to take advantage of the helpless, some use it for their gain, some use it as leverage, etc.

The relationship that you so desire must be built in your mind before it makes its way to reality. As you very well know, everything you have or do will be formed as a thought, first.

19ᵗʰ Type of Person to Avoid

Avoid People Who Lack Self-Control

Satisfaction and fulfillment come from the inside out, not the other way around. However, if satisfaction and fulfillment are attained from the outside in, one must then ask the question according to Jeremiah 13:23, "Can the Ethiopian change his skin or the leopard its spots? Then may you also do good who are accustomed to doing evil."

Of course, this is not a bible study session; however, this goes to show that we are who we are, for a reason. And there is no reason to sugar-coat an image that's destined to be. In my opinion, if you have ever told a lie, you have the potential to cheat. If you've ever gotten bored with your spouse, mate or partner, you have the potential to cheat. If you've been hurt by your spouse, mate or partner, you have the potential to cheat. If you've ever been lonely, you have the potential to cheat, and the list goes on. Now, hear me well, everyone has a sensitive spot. However, just because there is a sensitive spot of potential, it does not necessarily mean that it will take place unless you put some action behind it.

Once a cheater, always a cheater comes to mind when a person tells me that they have been delivered from cheating. Some may agree that you can be delivered from cheating, but I personally disagree. We all have a cheater within; meaning that there is temptation in every woman, and there is temptation in every man that lays dormant until it's awakened. Once this happens, it will sneak up on you like a leopard in the night. Now that we have that established, we can indeed be delivered from the **act** of cheating, but the temptation will still reside within the soul. I am not in the business to bash people who cheat, nor am I here to proclaim that I am a saint. However, I am here to show you how easy it is for someone to get caught with their pants down:

Late one morning, Hector decided that he was going to spend his Saturday morning watching television while his girlfriend Maria did laundry. After Maria left to go to the Laundromat, he quickly changed his mind and ended up going to his cousin's house to play pool. While Hector was hanging out with his cousin, Maria called to let him know that she was going to stop by her mom's for a while. Hector decides to go by Kim's house to get some loving because he knows that Maria hangs out at her mom's for at least 3 hours. Hector had Maria's schedule down; he knew exactly where she was, at all times.

When Maria got back from her mom's house, she greeted Hector like usual, but for some odd reason, she tasted something sweet on his lips. She did not say anything at that time; she just waited around until he went to sleep to check his underwear. This confirms a woman's intuition; his underwear was definitely stained, big time. She called her mom sobbing, and her mom told her not to confront him about something that she could not prove. Her mom also told her that if she starts looking for poop, she's going to find it. All she needed to do was to keep her mouth closed, pray and pay attention. Maria prayed and fasted for 7 days; she still treated Hector pleasant as she asked for God's guidance. One day after work, Maria locked her keys in the car, she called Hector for the duplicate key, and he was nowhere to be found. She finally had to call a locksmith to get the car open.

As soon as she gets home, Hector walks in the house as if he had a hard day at work. She kissed him and tasted the same sweet taste on his lips again. So, this time, she decided to give him a big hug, as she took a sniff to smell the scent of his skin. A woman's intuition again, he smells a little too sweet to have been working all day at the factory. Hector eventually checked his messages, and then he realized that Maria had been calling him while he was at Kim's place. He did not know what type of lie he was going to tell, but he knew that he had to come up with a good one. He went into the kitchen with a puppy-dog face trying to explain to Maria what happened. Maria politely said, "There is no reason to lie when you have brought the evidence home with you." He said, "What do you mean by that." She responded, "The least you could have done is wipe her strawberry lip gloss off your lips. Oh, by the way, tell your girlfriend that Caress Body Wash is not made for men." Hector was shocked; he did not think Maria was that smart. To her amazement, he began to tell her about Kim. He explained how he was really in love with her and that he's relieved that she knows his secret. He doesn't have to walk around with this heavy burden of guilt. Maria told him to get his stuff and to go live with Kim. Hector packed a few things and left.

One week later, Hector came by with Kim to pick up the rest of his things. When Maria opened the door and saw that he brought Kim to her house, she went crazy. She could not hold her composure; she started yelling at Hector; Kim jumps into the argument, then a fight breaks out between Maria and Kim. As Hector tried to break up the fight, Kim's wig gets pulled off. Maria stopped dead in her tracks; she now realizes that Kim is not a woman. Kim is a man!

Maria broke down; she could not believe that Hector left her for another man. She looked at Hector and asked him why. He said that he was born that way. Once again, Kim jumps into the conversation and tells Maria, "Since Hector thinks that you are so smart, you had a piece of me too. It was not strawberry lip gloss that you tasted on his lips. It was sweet strawberry flavored Kama Sutra that came from my body." Maria began to vomit. She did not want to hear it anymore; she could no longer bear the thought of Hector not even brushing his teeth or cleaning his mouth after licking on another man!

Maria finally got up off the floor, told Hector and Kim to get out of her house and that she would have his things shipped to his cousin's house.

Maria cannot look at men the same again; and, for that reason, she is still seeking counseling. Hector is still going both ways and is now cheating on Kim with another woman. Unmet needs provoke the cheater from within across the board, whether we are heterosexual, bisexual, homosexual, or transsexual. When we feel as if we are lacking something, dissatisfied with something, or rejected in some way, it's in our nature to seek comfort. Whether that comfort is physical, mental, emotional, or spiritual, it's all comfort. However, in our moment of seeking comfort, we determine whether our actions become positive or negative, hurtful or soothing, perverted or non-perverted, etc.

20th Type of Person to Avoid

Avoid People Who Cannot Be Honest

Understanding is the best way to tame the cheater from within, as well as the cheater within someone else. If you bash cheaters, do you really think that your spouse, mate, or partner would tell you if he or she cheated or is tempted to cheat? More than likely, he or she will not until they are caught; by then, the damage is already done. Not only that, when we have an understanding of our mate's wants, needs, and desires, we are better able to fulfill them.

The number 1 rule to taming the cheater from within is to understand what triggers the urge to cheat. In order to truly understand the trigger, we must take the time to understand our behavioral patterns associated with the process of cheating. As a result, we become better able to pinpoint the release of the cheater from within; therefore, allowing us to exercise self-control. Actually, once we gain control over ourselves to properly understand our trigger points, then we are able to find the source.

Our ability to find the source of our trigger points is really based on our value and belief system of our:

1. Sexual Addictions.
2. Traditional (Family) Addictions.
3. Emotional Addictions.
4. Drama Addictions.
5. Deception Addictions.
6. Passion Addictions.
7. Attention Addictions.

There is always a reason why we do what we do, and until we take the time to understand the underlying meaning of our actions, we will not change; unless, the pain of not changing supersedes the pain of making the transition to not cheat. Yes, the pain that's associated with taming the cheater has a way of taming the most sophisticated cheater.

Beverly somehow fell in love with Brad, who was a known Playboy. Brad did not make his Playboy mentality a secret, He had Playboy tattoos, Playboy accessories, he basically had Playboy everything. However, for some odd reason, Beverly subconsciously thought that she could change Brad into a good boy. As a result, Brad did fall in love with her, just as he fell in love with several other women the same week he met Beverly. She thought that her beauty was enough for Brad, but she was sadly mistaken as he began to introduce her to his other girlfriends.

She was devastated that she couldn't prevent him from cheating; as a result, she became tired of being Miss Goody Two Shoes. One day she made a commitment to herself that she was going to show him how it felt to be cheated on, even if that's the last thing that she did. Beverly began this process by using the law of detachment; she detached herself from Brad mentally, emotionally, and physically—meaning "NO SEX, NO CONVERSATION, and NO FUZZY WUZZY."

Beverly began to change her appearance; actually, she occupied her time by being at the gym, mall or hair salon, doing things for the betterment of herself, she no longer had time for Brad's disrespectful foolishness. She became very secretive; she did not discuss her personal life with Brad, nor did she have a desire to listen to his. When Brad calls, she used the 30-second rule—she could not hold a conversation with Brad over 30 seconds. She could not argue, fuss, fight, become angry or react to anything that Brad did or said; she could only use pleasant greetings while showering him with kindness. After a couple of months of this, Brad begged her for a date, and she stood him up several times; she chose to occupy her time with more beneficial friends! Is Beverly a good girl gone bad? Brad could not believe that the shoe was on the other foot.

He now understood how it really felt being played. The pain of him being thrown to the side by Beverly provoked the desire for him to change his ways. He begged Beverly to become his woman; she refused. He even proposed to her; she refused. The damage had already been done, and Beverly was not going to risk loving a newly reformed playboy. Even though Brad and Beverly did not get back together, she did indeed contribute to having Mr. Playboy Brad readjust his Playboy Mentality.

Brad is indeed a player at heart, but now he is a player with limits, boundaries, and respect. He is now a pastor and is faithfully married. He no longer engages in the act of cheating, but he must put that cheating spirit under subjection daily. Beverly is married as well; she has a wonderful husband that she met soon after she detached herself from Brad.

CHAPTER 4

The Roaring Wad

Our inner qualities are always on display whether we want them or not. Everything that we do, say, or become a part of, reveals certain things about our character and how we treat people as well. Yes, there are certain things that we may try to hide or need to hide; however, the moment we are put under pressure, what is inside of us will come out regardless of whether it is positive or negative. Our self-control or the lack thereof exposes our attitude, values, beliefs, desires, education, essence, and habits that are basically transparent in 4 areas:

1. Body language.
2. Tone of Voice.
3. Non-verbal Communication.
4. Verbal Communication.

We have all complained about something, and we are all

selfish to a certain extent when it comes down to our own well-being; however, conditional selfishness destroys more relationships than we would ever care to imagine. Actually, when we place too many conditions on our relationships with people, places, and things without analyzing ourselves, we then step over the line into envy and jealousy. Furthermore, everyone is not for everybody; however, with everyone that enters our lives will have a lesson or an experience attached to it. Whether we embrace the experience or ignore it is definitely up to us. For those who are all up in our face nagging or provoking us............we must take it serious, clicking the AVOID button.

21st Type of Person to Avoid

Avoid People Who Nag

We must address the naggers, and now a day, they are universal. We will also find that a nag will naturally chase their mate away. The face value of patience resides within us all until we allow impatience to rule over us. Nagging and complaining are two things that destroy relationships, drive people away, or cause people to seek refuge. However, if a couple is driven by the drama, then this may work for them; but, I am not here to entertain the "Jerry Springer Relationships" anyway. I am here to inspire those who are ready to take their relationship to another level. A nagger is the most conditional person that we would ever want to

Chapter 4 | Ruby Fleurcius

meet. As long as they are getting what they want, they are happy. The minute that they do not get what they want, then there is another set of rules to follow. Of course, a nagger would not reveal this information to anyone; but if we are a nagger, deep down within our heart, we know this is the truth. Just remember, whether we are a nagger or a naggee, whatever we ignore out of jealousy, anger, or envy, gets repeated, simply ask Nick:

Everyone wants to have their cake and eat it every now and again. However, Nick is a man who took having his cake and eating it too—to a whole new level.

*After having literally over **100** relationships under his belt, he met Ivey. She was a country girl that believed in men respecting women. Her mother would always say, "You are able to determine how a man would treat you by the way he treats his mother." And, every guy that she dated, she never experienced a man mistreating his mother, until she met Nick.*

She would always tell him that he could not talk to his mother that way, and that it was not nice. He would always say, "I take care of my mom, I would give her the world; but, this is how I am, and I am going to be me." However, Ivey believed that God could change anybody, including Nick. She always had the hope that one day he would finally treat his mother better. After years of hanging out with Nick, he began to treat her the same way he treated his mom. She confronted him about verbally abusing her and his response was, "What make you think that I would treat you better than my mother?" Ivey should have walked away that day; but, she overlooked it, hoping that he would one day return the kindness and respect that she's always shown to him.

As their friendship continued, Ivey was viciously beaten and raped by her ex. This was a very tragic moment in Ivey's life, and she did not know who to turn to; so she kept this incident to herself, hoping that it would just go away. Well, it did not go away, as a result of her rape, she became pregnant. This time, she turned to Nick for emotional support and now, she regrets confiding in him at all. Instead of Nick supporting her after this traumatic event, he crucified her. He sought the advice of others while dragging her name through the dirt as he laughed and made jokes about it. He took that sensitive moment in her life and dogged her out with his words. His tongue became a double-edged sword, cutting wounds into Ivey's broken heart making her feel as if it was her fault for her ex- taking advantage of her.

Ivey really understands how date rape goes unreported by many women. It's embarrassing to be taken advantage of; on the other hand, it's more embarrassing to be accused of allowing it to happen. Ivey never told anyone how Nick treated her and how he would yell at her, cussing her out causing her to become an emotional mess. She was so stressed out as it began to cause complications in her pregnancy. After having a nagging conversation with Nick, her pressure would skyrocket, putting her and the baby in danger. She was in and out of the hospital as the undue stress began to kill her, she did not know what to do, and she did not know who to talk to anymore. All she knew is that she was at the lowest point of her life, and all she needed was a little encouragement.

As Ivey held in the pain of the entrapment of her ex and the constant crucifixion by Nick, her condition would no longer allow her to continue this way as she went into premature labor, only to lose her child. Yes, the stress associated with being nagged caused her to lose her child; she could not believe that stress would make her body do abnormal things. Even though she had to go through that ordeal, she never blamed anyone because she became stronger and wiser than ever. Amazingly, during this ultimate time of loss and regret, she knew that she still had a choice to live. She began to trust and believe in God like never before, while keeping all the nagging people at arm's length.

Nick is doing his thing and looking for a wife; of course, he still loves women, going through 30 more women since the ordeal with Ivey. Ivey has forgiven her ex, and she has forgiven Nick as well. She's still friends with both. She feels very strongly that they both made her the strong woman that she is today. She has a strong testimony about how to love, how to forgive, and how to let go. Ivey knows what she wants out of a man, and she will not allow anyone to nag, crucify, or disrespect the great woman that God created her to be.

Great relationships begin with trust and continue with positive affirmations. We must look for the good in all things in order for our relationships to thrive in greatness. I have found that men have big egos; but, for some odd reason, women possess even bigger egos. This is not about who has the biggest ego; it's about feeding the ego the right type of food. However, a word of caution, the more an ego is broken or insulted, we put ourselves at an even greater risk of being cheated on. In so many words, the more we insult a person openly, the more we risk being cheated on secretly. The fleeting desires to become a slave to our ego can and will inhibit our ability to listen and learn. As we all know, a wise person will listen more than he or she will speak. For that reason, it is imperative that we bridle our tongues while learning and preparing ourselves to go to the next level in life.

22nd Type of Person to Avoid

Avoid People Who Are Stuck On Negative

Who likes to be criticized? Absolutely no one; however, when we are knowingly or unknowingly sensitive to criticism, we tend to become easily offended. This is basically a form of "silent hurt" that usually goes unheard of or unnoticed until someone brings it to the forefront of our lives. For those who appear to be on top of their game, busted egos create an alter-ego personality in those who are constantly picked-on or talked about. When a person gets tired of the nagging, we will find that they will:

- Begin spending more time away from home.
- Work more without an increase in income.
- They begin to avoid having contact with the nagger.
- They will suddenly start hiding their phone.
- They will start ignoring calls.
- They will start having little or no Sex.
- They will start saying, "I need more."
- They will start the comparison process.
- They will start becoming confused about what they tell you.
- They will start to always feel tired.

- They will avoid eye contact
- They will begin to limit their conversations.
- They may become fidgety, stuttering, scratching, or yawning when spoken to.
- They will begin to hang out with friends of the opposite sex.
- They may begin to start sleeping with another person.
- They will begin to have private conversations.
- They will begin to lack interest.
- He or she will start saying, "I need space."
- He or she will stop wearing a wedding ring.

We do not have to be heard all the time, but being a nagger is not the way to go. When we speak, speak the truth in love, while choosing our words carefully with a positive outlook, and we will always find the right words to say at the right time, even when we are rubbed the wrong way.

23rd Type of Person to Avoid

Avoid People Who Are Hypocrites

I am not going to preach to the choir about hypocrites—I am just going to expose the things that we don't readily talk about much. Our divorce rate says that 80% of marriages are ending in divorce. Why? Relationship Hypocrisy, we have become driven by power, money, and sex. We have become a slave to society; the ones that do not have, cannot become a part of the elite groups of people, until their income level changes, social status changes, or they become sexually controlled by the elite pimps. Now, as we deal with the sex trance at hand, if an individual does not have money or status, but is willing to use sex as a tool or weapon to obtain money, power, status, a dinner, a movie, or just to make ends meet, it is indeed a form of prostitution. I am not just talking about the prostitution that takes place on the street corners, I am referring to the undercover sex slaves that sit next to us on the job, in the church, in the pulpit, lives next door to us, or maybe lives in our own house with us—who knows, the list goes on! Also, undercover sex slaves are not just limited to females—in today's time, men are selling out faster than females to get what they want. Although we do not like hearing the truth, it does not surprise me about what we will, or will not do behind closed doors! We are quick to judge others for selling their souls to the devil, sliding down a pole in the strip clubs, or selling/using drugs to name a few; but, when it comes down to power, money, or sex—we do not know what we would do until our back is up against the wall. Make no mistake about it; positively or negatively, everyone has a story, and everyone has a price! A price that they would pay, or a price they would not pay for power, money, or sex; as well as a story to justify their behavior.

24th Type of Person to Avoid

Avoid People Who Kill The Dreams Of Others

I have found that there are two obvious signs that our soul is in utter chaos: 1. If we are a person who has everything, who is not happy, and is always on the take, while crucifying others for not living up to their expectation. 2. If we are a person who has nothing, who doesn't want anything and prides himself/herself on crucifying others for wanting more out of life; or better yet, a person who enjoys killing the dreams of others to keep them at their level or in a box. Nevertheless, I have also found that to maximize our understanding of the relationships; we cannot allow outside appearances, circumstances, or events that are related to power, money, or sex to interfere with our instincts. Yes, I said INSTINCTS! This is one major element of who we are that gets ignored the most—we can instinctively do, create, and become if we simply allow our instincts to take its rightful place to weed out people who hide their negative characteristics under a mask. By doing so, it will allow joy, peace, patience, kindness, goodness, generosity, gentleness, faithfulness, modesty, and self-control to enter our lives to give us a conscience worth having, as well as showing off.

25th Type of Person to Avoid

Avoid People With Anger Problems

Who doesn't become angry from time-to-time? We all will; however, anger that's used to manipulate others or to have our way is another issue that needs to be dealt with accordingly. When we find ourselves controlling others with our anger, we will also find that we have placed limits on our ability to effectively communicate; therefore, creating strife in our Relationship. Relational strife does not solve problems; actually, it creates them. Until we realize what we are doing, we will continue to operate in a selfishness that creates a snare of our own making.

Overriding a person's will with anger is a recipe that brings about secret revenge, withdrawal, or rebellion. When we allow miscommunication to reign in our lives, we will find ourselves alienated from the people who are close to us or the people we work with daily. We cannot get mad at people for not doing what we want them to do; regardless of whether he or she is our husband/wife, girlfriend/boyfriend, child, friend, employee/employer, etc. Certainly, there are times when we need to exercise tough love; but, tough love has nothing to do with manipulative anger. Now, without a doubt, we may suffer the consequences and repercussions for not doing what we need to do; however, exercising discipline out of anger is not a justifiable action. Actually, it only justifies us to think through our anger and to make a decision out of correction and not control.

An unknown author once said, "Anger is one letter short of danger." I personally, stay away from individuals who are angry all the time. For me, it's like a time bomb waiting to happen. Whether your anger is kept a secret or whether it is well known, it must be controlled and dealt with accordingly. This will ensure that it does not manifest something that will cause harm to you or deprive you of your heart's desire. It's okay to cool-off before confronting a situation or circumstance that's derived out of anger. Besides, your best bet is to do and say things out of humble love and not anger to preserve a relationship that's worth keeping.

26th Type of Person to Avoid

Avoid People Who Refuse To Deal With Their Insecurities

When we refuse to deal with or acknowledge our fears and insecurities, it creates an emotional block of anger, strife, and unforgiveness that will cause chaos and confusion within our very own soul. When we switch-out on ourselves, it opens a string of deficiencies that becomes quite evident in our actions, our reactions, our attitude and how we live our lives. Furthermore, it is not necessary to sell ourselves short, when all we have to do is become rich in spirit and in truth. In so many words, when we become honest with ourselves about what we do, say, or think, we open the door to learning more about what we don't know without having to pretend as if we know everything. Once we become open to learning in spite of our insecurities, what we know will come across as wisdom through our humbleness and not overbearingness.

27th Type of Person to Avoid

Avoid People Who Constantly Relive Their Past

When we find ourselves holding on to the memories and pleasures of past relationships, we will find that we will tend to have more problems that contribute to our dissatisfaction. It is hard to have a relationship with someone we cannot communicate with; sooner or later someone will start complaining. Most of the time, complainers do whatever it takes to flatter others to get favors in return, only to find out that the complainer is never satisfied anyway. I have found that, when there is a complaint, there has already been a conceived thought of something better! If there was not a thought of something better, there would not be a complaint.

What's in the past is in the past! There is no need to bury ourselves in the things of old. Actually, it is the things of old that keep our heads buried in the sand of mental anguish. In a relationship, when we allow ourselves

Chapter 4 | Ruby Fleurcius

to become too mentally entangled in someone or something, rest assured that emotional bondage will soon follow like a thief in the night. Yes, most often it will take more than we are willing to give. However, our willingness to put away dead things gives us the power to cope and eliminate our sensitivities of being misunderstood. Every day provides us with an opportunity to live better than we did the day before. When we allow ourselves to live in victory, we then open the door to succeed in places that we never knew existed.

28th Type of Person to Avoid

Avoid People Who Are Insensitive or Rude

In order to maximize our relationship with others, we must become thoughtful and sensitive to their wants or needs, regardless of how far-fetched they may appear. When we positively exude our care and attention to those who are important to us, we will find that they respond better; plus, we put ourselves in a better position to have this reciprocated as well. There is no need to be rude or insensitive about anything….all we have to do is communicate effectively.

Using vulgar language is not necessary when trying to communicate; in my opinion, it is when we are at a loss of words that we have to resort to that type of language. When building a relationship, it is imperative that we are very careful about what comes out of our mouth. Remember, there is life and death in the power of the tongue; therefore, speak life into your relationship and life will come out of it. If you curse your relationship, that's what you will get as well—BEWARE! So, the next time you think that using vulgar language is the "IN" thing, think again. What you speak over yourself, your life, or your relationship is what you will attract to you in due time. It doesn't matter whether you use the word "cussing" or "cursing", they are both the same thing with the same amount of impact.

Insensitivity and rudeness are NOT characteristics that will build a solid relationship without someone getting their feelings hurt. In the midst of loving who you love, it's imperative to exercise extreme caution when dealing with someone who has the potential to emotionally or mentally traumatize you with their spoken words.

29th Type of Person to Avoid

Avoid People Who Are Constantly Looking For Your Faults

Harping on the faults of others to force them to change will cease to empower them to do so. Forcing people to do that in which they choose not to do is not a great way to get things done. Actually, we can accomplish more by empowering people and not forcing them. Power struggles are usually created when a person seemingly in charge use fault-finding tactics to knowingly or unknowingly manipulate others. Fault-finding does not bring about change; it brings about rebellion. As a matter of fact, when there is a sensitive place in a person's life, they will listen a lot more when they do not feel violated or threatened. Yes, there will be areas of our lives that we may need to acknowledge and work on; however, self-degradation or the degradation of others is not necessary.

When we share information without pointing the finger, we can accomplish more than we could ever imagine. When we are able to choose, it gives us the freedom to exercise our mind and think our own thoughts. Trust me, it's hard to go wrong sharing positive information with options. However, if someone is constantly telling you more about what's wrong with you, and not what's RIGHT about you—it's a possibility that you may need to have a heart-to-heart conversation or pump the brakes on that relationship before it's too late.

30th Type of Person to Avoid

Avoid People Who Are Very Impatient With You

Patience is designed to keep our emotions under control and the minute we become impatient, it causes our emotions to begin racing out of control. A secretly impatient person is often found out through their inability to control their emotions. Of course, we are all emotional beings, and it is our responsibility to set the tone for what, who, why, and how we reveal our emotions. And if we don't set the tone, then our emotions will do it for us!

Our emotions have been and still are one of the biggest contributors to the downfall of the relationships between men and women. If we do not want to become a statistic, then we must find a way to control our emotions to better control our relationships. The code of patience is to be careful about making decisions when you are emotional; and, to be careful about becoming emotional when making decisions. This will definitely keep your mind clear about what you are thinking, doing, or becoming involved in. When you break this code of patience, you will find that bad decisions are made when they could have been avoided. And if you are dealing with someone who does not have time for you, who is very impatient with you, or who is always in a hurry, that is a tell-tale sign that they have other things going on that takes precedence over you. Therefore, you must reevaluate that situation before it's too late.

31st Type of Person to Avoid

Avoid People Who Talk About You

People will be people, and they are going to talk regardless of what we do, say, or become. However, what I am really talking about here, are the back-stabbing, two-faced people that we need to avoid. The ones that are all in our face to gather up information about what's going on in our lives, only to talk about us behind our back—yes, that one, AVOID them! As a rule of thumb, in outright integrity, we should never say anything about someone that we are not willing to say to them face-to-face. Therefore, if something proceeds out of the gate of our mouth, and we would never say that to that individual that we are speaking of, then it's a possibility that we should not be saying that. Is this gossip? In my opinion, it's beyond gossip, this is a back-stabber, BEWARE.

There are times when we become stressed by the issues of life; but we cannot forget about the things that we have worked so hard to attain. Regardless of whether we are the criticizer or the criticizee, when we are in a relationship, we are not a one-man's show, and we need to love each other, respecting each other's differences! We need people, and people need us; besides, what do we gain from talking about someone negatively or backstabbing them? Okay, I will reveal what we will gain; w e will gain frustration, depression, anxiety, feeling sorry for ourselves, resentfulness, helplessness, and the list goes on with negative attributes. Once consumed by these emotions, self-destruction is around the corner waiting for us to give in, bringing back to our own house what we are dishing out. Karma is in full effect; therefore, we must be careful about the company we keep and ever so mindful about the people we avoid as well. Furthermore, when we look to judge someone for what's going on in their household, just remember that we are also bringing judgment to our own back door; and, when it comes down to this judgment thing, we can fool a lot of people, but we can't fool ourselves!

32nd Type of Person to Avoid

Avoid People Who Are Not Compassionate

Compassion will remove the anxious desire to become angry or the desire to nag your spouse, partner, or mate. The frustrations of life are designed to keep you off balance. You know better than anyone else what triggers you to become angry, and not compassionate. Just remember, you do have a choice! Everyone will become angry at some point; however, in order to overcome anger, it has to be replaced with something positive, such as compassion—that is indeed what's needed to empower and strengthen you to forgive and let go of the desire to stay angry. This may be your test or the deciding factor of whether or not you build or destroy your own relationship.

Who are we behind closed doors? I must agree that most of us put our best face forward when we are in the public eye, pretending to be someone or something that we are not; and then again, some of us just let it all hangout, so to speak! However, our goal is to become like minded in all

Chapter 4 | Ruby Fleurcius

our ways. When we are not like-minded in all our ways, we will find the disruption evident in our actions, reactions, conversations, waywardness, and the way we browbeat others for the same things that we ourselves are guilty of. Of course, no one is perfect; however, if we do not show compassion, if we do not show understanding, if we do not forgive, if we are hateful, if we are selfish, if we are demeaning, if we are ungrateful, if we are a trouble-maker, or if we are too arrogant, we will find that these self-defying behaviors will begin to break down the foundation in our own house. A house with a shaky foundation, a house without walls, a house that leaves the door open, a house without a roof, and a house without a Spiritual Relationship with God will become a problematic household by default. When our house becomes prone to problems, we will begin to look for things on the outside to fill the void, opposed to bringing some sort of resolve to the situation, circumstance, or event. In order to build the best relationship ever, you must offer encouragement to yourself and others, while making your house a home by focusing, building, and maintaining your own house without condemning others for that in which they have chosen to do behind closed doors. If someone is not bringing kindness, love, and peace to your home, it is a possibility that you need to show them to the door.

33rd Type of Person to Avoid

Avoid People Who Are Very Confrontational

Run from a Hellion on Wheels. If you are in a relationship with someone that looks for trouble or fights all the time, RUN. If you do not, you will become like them in due time—it's like quicksand, it will suck you under when you least expect it. You know exactly when someone is exhibiting trifling behavior; and, if it goes ignored, you will be drawn in by default.

What do you do when peace is boring to a hell-raiser and hell-raising is repulsive to a person of peace? The answer is, "Back Away." We cannot change what people are accustomed to, nor do we want to compromise our integrity. There is no reason to get upset with people who do not understand us, and we cannot beat ourselves up for not understanding others—that's just a part of life.

People, places, and things come into your life for a reason; and, they will also exit your life for a reason as well, especially if you know what you want and do not want in your life. If you are serious about building quality relationships, take a moment to evaluate what you are going to allow in your circle or who needs to leave it. By doing so, this will enable you to make the right moves at the right time to protect yourself, your environment, your job, your family/friends and most of all, your sanity. Just remember, a positive attitude will enable you to discover incredible opportunities that will enhance your life for the better.

Chapter 4 | Ruby Fleurcius

34th Type of Person to Avoid

Avoid People Who Do Not Listen

How can you get your spouse, mate, children, friend, or co-worker to listen to you? Well, my first question to you is, "Are you listening to them?" Effective communication is the golden key in any conversation regardless of whether it is someone you know or don't know. We can have someone talking all day until they are blue in the face, but if they are not getting through to those that they are communicating with, then there is a problem somewhere. When people develop a deaf ear to us, it is a possibility that we are missing the mark of something that we may have taken for granted. In my opinion, we can yield better results when we genuinely speak to someone about a situation, circumstance, or event; opposed to speaking **AT** them or **ABOUT** them to their face.

The way we start a conversation will usually determine how it will end; therefore, when we are building and maintaining relationships, we must think before we speak. This is a vital resource needed to be able to get our point across without using words that will hurt others. Listening is one way to silently encourage others without having to persuade them to unwillingly see what we see. It is important to learn when to speak and when to listen. The right words at the right time will encourage them; but on the other hand, the wrong words at the wrong time can discourage and damage them for a lifetime.

Some people are more sensitive than others, and some people are just indifferent. In spite of how a person is perceived, an encouraging word WILL pierce the heart of the most sensitive to the most rock solid person. In the process of listening, we must be able to listen to ourselves and others without passing judgment. If possible, try to reframe from offering your opinion until it's asked for—just sympathize, relate, and move on. Most often, people will tell you how to communicate on their level, and they will tell you how they would like to be treated, but you must LISTEN to what they are saying. And, you must also pay attention to what they are not saying through their body language.

The words that we choose when speaking are a reflection of who we are. Often enough, we hear that our eyes are the window to our soul; however, we do not hear that what comes out of our mouth gives us a sneak peek at what we are thinking and feeling. If we desire to know where someone's head is at, simply listen to what's coming out of their mouth. Now, on the flip side of things, if we do not desire for someone to know where our head is at, it is better to keep our lips zipped. In order to build a powerhouse relationship, you must become a good steward over what comes out of your mouth, and think about what you are saying before you say it—you never know who is listening. Besides, choosing your words carefully will give you an opportunity to safeguard the contents of your heart.

Chapter 4 | Ruby Fleurcius

35th Type of Person to Avoid

Avoid People Who Doubt Everything About You

We have no room for a doubting Thomas in our lives. In my opinion, it is imperative to have someone who will help to keep the focus in a relationship and not take from it. Doubt is the breeding ground of justification and rationalization that provoke this wonderful thing called EXCUSES. Excuses, excuses, excuses—everybody has one, especially when they are trying to justify what they are doing, saying, or becoming. Whenever we make an excuse about something or someone, doubt has the opportunity to lay the groundwork of mixed feelings. Of course, with mixed feelings, here comes the emotional roller-coaster creating a domino effect in our lives. If a person is bold enough to do, say, or become something—they should OWN it; and, that would definitely leave little room for doubt, mixed feelings, and the emotional roller-coaster. Own up to what you are doing, saying, or becoming—this is the only way to free yourself from living a lie, put your doubts to rest, and live up to your greatest potential, while avoiding those who try to place doubt in your heart.

A crystal clear perspective about our mishaps and setbacks in life leaves little room for doubt. When we have a crystal clear perspective about our lives, it does not necessarily mean that we have all the answers. What it means is that we are able to trust life to create a magnetic force of our beliefs. For example, if you believe that everything happens for a reason—then life will avail itself to reveal the reason to you. Now, whether you believe that reason is a stepping-stone, or a set-back is totally up to you.

When our perspective is foggy, it has a way of preventing us from clearly envisioning the desires of our heart. In so many words, we become confused or doubtful about our wants and needs in life; therefore, settling for temporary comfort that ends in the appearance of a setback, failure, affair, broken relationship, or divorce.

As simple as it may seem, it is extremely hard for others to understand and relate to us when we don't understand how to relate to ourselves effectively. Often enough, it's in our nature to want people to understand our wants, needs, and desires; but, if we lack the understanding of our own wants, needs, and desires, then we set ourselves up for our own disappointment. Your best bet is to know and understand what you want, need, and desire in and out of a relationship, leaving little or no room for doubt to have its way in your life. This will ensure that you are able to please yourself, while pleasing those that you are in relations with as well. Therefore, setting the groundwork for a great, fulfilling relationship that's built on the trust and confidence of knowing you have their best interest at heart. Bo knows about this all too well:

"Bo was a good guy who came home every night faithfully. As a matter of fact, Bo was a God fearing man who believed in taking care of his family. Two years into the relationship with his wife, May, she

began to nag about simple little things such as taking the garbage out, cooking, cleaning the house, and taking care of their 1-year-old. Bo did not complain; he did not mind taking care of his child and his wife; however, he did have a problem with his wife sitting home all day watching the soaps, talking with her friends and doing nothing. This went on for several years, as Bo continued to work his full-time job, cooking, cleaning, and taking care of his child; yet, he still did not complain, even though he was torn and tortured from within. And, regardless of how he may have felt, pleasing his wife was his 1st priority.

When his child became old enough to go to preschool, instead of May staying home or finding a job, she went off with her friends all day. However, she did pick their son up from preschool and dropped him at home with Bo, only to leave again. She came home around 8 p.m. every night with no explanation. She never spent time with the family, so Bo became a little concerned with her behavior. One day, Bo gained enough courage to question her activity; she became irate, stormed out of the house and did not come home for several days. Of course, Bo felt as if she was seeing someone else, but he was in denial. May did not cook, clean or do anything for her husband; she showed no interest whatsoever. Bo wanted to preserve their marriage because it was the Godly thing to do until he realized that she was spending all of their money shopping, drinking, and having fun.

May had totally lost respect for her husband because she felt as if he was boring and weak. Low and behold, one day she brought their son home from preschool, and she never came back. She left Bo and their child without saying, "Good-bye." Bo searched for his wife for days, he even reported her missing, only to find out that she spent their savings to buy a new home for her and her boyfriend of 6 years. She had been seeing her boyfriend for the entire duration of their marriage. Bo was astounded and deeply hurt. He could not believe that she left *him, and their child broke, busted and disgusted. As a result, he began to hate God for allowing this to happen to him.*

He had lost respect for all women; as a matter of fact, he made a promise to himself that he would never allow a woman to hurt him again. Bo became a womanizer, even though he regained his respect for women, he never allowed them to get close to his heart. And, if he started to develop feelings for a specific woman, he would sever the relationship. As Bo continued to raise his son, his son became accustomed to him dating several women at a time. And, when his son went to middle school, he began to experience an adrenaline rush of having more than one girlfriend at a time. By the time he was in high school, he could not count the amount of women that he had gone through. Bo's son began to produce a mirror image of his actions."

All too often, the actions of one person can produce a domino effect for generations to come. Bo is still single and loving it, and his son is married with 2 children while discreetly cheating on his wife. May has been married & divorced 4 times; she is now battling the Aids virus and homeless. Can anything good come of this?

36th Type of Person to Avoid

Avoid People Who Are Ineffective

A constant following of ineffectiveness can and will cause the best of us to reevaluate our attitude, actions, and reactions, especially when the results are right in front of us. As the same negative cycle continues, when we misappropriate our time, we will experience a higher level of stress, extreme fatigue, disrupted time with our family, strained relationships, and/or a constant bout with failure. If someone is constantly screwing up things, there is a bigger problem at hand, and one must decide if that's what they would like to constantly deal with in a relationship. If it is not, one must avoid cleaning up the messes of a grown person.

In my opinion, time is of the essence; therefore, it must be managed in order to maximize it, or we will not get anything done. For me, I simply determine the when, where, how, and why's of what's important by making a physical or mental list, and determine in advance what needs to get done first, and what can be dropped. Once I begin my day, I limit the amount of distractions that I will allow into my space to ensure that I do not waste time, or break my flow with people, places, and things that will take me in a direction that is not conducive. I am not saying that we will not have distractions, because we will—our best bet is to train our minds in advance to deal with the distractions; therefore, we are better able to deal with the biggest time-wasters such as chatting on the phone, gossiping, texting, watching too much television, gaming, FaceBooking, etc.

I have found through my own personal experiences that the difference between an effective or ineffective person is TIME MANAGEMENT. When we are busy accomplishing nothing is a big slap in the face, especially if we have nothing to show for it. In building quality relationships, you must make time management your first priority, focusing on getting results and not just being busy—this will definitely help you accomplish more in the allotted time given. Plus, you can't go wrong increasing your effectiveness and reducing unnecessary stress to increase your productivity; therefore, giving you more quality time to relax, and enjoy life with the people, places, and things you love.

CHAPTER 5

Relationship Wisdom Roar

A person that value their relationships take pride in themselves, their home, their family, their career, their friends, setting priorities, helping the needy, and their spiritual relationship. A person of this caliber wears many hats, and they do not mind effectively balancing the people, places, and things that are valuable to them, while exhibiting great character to all that they come in contact with. If we would like to possess the characteristics of this type of individual, we must start with our attitude. This is the deal breaker between effective relationships and our circle.

As a person who pride myself on building effective relationships, I do not proclaim to be perfect, nor is anyone perfect; but, when a person proclaims to be a good person, I check to see how they treat their spouse, children, relatives, friends, coworkers, and then others—in that order. Trust me, it's a dead giveaway on the level of integrity one possesses from within. If someone treats people on the outside who are not related to them better than they treat their spouse, children, and family—there are some deep rooted issues that need to be resolved.

In a relationship, your attitude, skills, and talents that you possess will do 3 things:

- Build people, places, and things.
- Destroy people, places, and things.
- Allow you to pick up debris causing you to become a victim of circumstance.

Your attitude, thoughts, and actions will be the determining factor in whether you build, destroy, or pick up debris. However, if you want lasting success in relationships, you must continue to build yourself, and the lives of others without expecting anything in return. If not, one will find a long trail of irreconcilably broken, chaotic relationships. These types of relationships are a very touchy subject; however, I am going to give one the information needed to overcome these types of obstacles.

If chaos seems to follow an individual, it is due to conditioning, due to their environment, or due to the fact that they are covering up the pain that they are feeling from within. This doesn't mean that a chaotic person is a bad person; it only means that they are hurting and cannot make the pain go away, so they use chaos as a sedative. If chaos begins to come your way, simply zip your lips to ensure that you do not become a sedative for someone else's unresolved pain or unresolved issues.

37th Type of Person to Avoid

Avoid People Who Block Your Creativity

We can become creative if we recognize our unique talents and develop mastery in those areas. Of course, that doesn't guarantee that the world will recognize us, but it does provide the soul satisfaction that comes with living a creative life. There is an abundance of untapped wealth that's hidden inside of you. How do you get to it? It's so easy, just simply become aware of it. It does not matter what you have or do not have, your hidden treasure is just waiting for you to share it with the world, and everything else will work itself out. You are designed with many different levels of creativity that will support the life of your own choosing. Surround yourself with people who love and support you—you will find that you will become even more creative. Spend time meditating on your own worthiness, reading about other creative people, creative solutions, and the positive power of your own creative forces.

Well, how do you turn a negative situation into a positive one? Easy, change the way you think! You have the power to change your thoughts like you change the channel on your television. I call it "**vujá dé**." It means to change your perspective. You do not need a miracle in order to find, reveal, or maximize your talents—you are the miracle. No, you will not be able to save the world, but you can transform YOUR part of the world. Just start focusing on what you do best and be the best at what you do using what you have collected over the years or what you have left. In my opinion, you determine your worth when you assess the value of your intangible assets that you possess from within. Tangible assets become worthless when you make excuses for not knowing its value. In so many words, the things that you cannot see have far more value than the things that you can see. I know that it's hard to imagine, but it's the truth! No more excuses, if I can do it, you can too.

38th Type of Person to Avoid

Avoid People Who Put You In A Box

In a Relationship you must become a treasure chest of creativity to put your fear on the back burner, pulling your dreams, desires, or passions to the forefront. The turnaround in your relationship that you are looking for will be determined by your ability to become creative with what you have right now. It is also composed of doing the things that you already know you should be doing. Simply think outside the box, around the box, and through the box with a different approach. Is it that simple? Yes. That's exactly why you cannot allow someone to place you in a box, limiting your potential…..check out this story with Casey and her power play:

Casey is a very smart, intelligent accountant who owns a very high profile accounting firm. One day, what appeared to be the man of her dreams, walk through the front door. He was so handsome that she could not keep her eyes off of him. If you believe in love at first sight, that did it for Casey. He swept her off of her feet without him even knowing it. She knew that she had to get to know this man, and she did not care if he was married or not; she had to have him.

After a few minutes of doing her breathing exercise, Casey grows balls and walks up to him and said, "I have to have you." He says, "Okay, when do you want me." She responded, "Tonight, pick me up at 8, here's my address." He says, "Wow. I'll be there." Casey strutted back to her office with a smile on her face. Steve got to Casey's house on time with flowers in hand, and greeted her as if he had known her more than a few hours. Casey did not feel that he could really love her without having sex with her, so she did not waste any time; she turned on some music and got busy. She was just like her mom; she had no shame in her game. Casey had more uncles than a person could shake a stick at. As a matter of fact, she remembered her mom introducing her to 4 new uncles in one month; but for some odd reason, Casey never saw her uncles more than once.

As Steve became a little more acquainted with Casey, he saw an opportunity to use her knowledge to build his dream. She was okay with helping him, and she did not mind sharing her mental capabilities, besides she wanted to contribute to his success in hopes of being his wife one day. After working diligently with Steve for several months building his business, Shelly, Steve's wife comes into Casey's office requesting to see her. Casey had been seeing Steve for almost a year and never once asked about his marital status, nor did he tell her. Shelly began to speak with Casey about her affair with her husband and how much she was hurt by it.

Casey began to sympathize with her as she began to apologize for the role that she had been playing in Steve's life. In a way, Shelly began to trust Casey because she felt as if she was a victim as well. Shelly even went to the extent of telling Casey that she and Steve were trying to have a baby. It was a moment of gruesome pain as she and Casey sobbed. Casey even went to the extent of telling her that she would not see her husband again and that she had nothing to worry about. They both did not mention anything about this meeting to Steve; however, Casey did continue to see him. She continued to work on his business, as he began to make 10 times more than he did in the previous years.

Several months later, Casey became really sick and went to her doctor; to her cunning amazement, she was pregnant. She became so excited as the doctor told her that she was pregnant with twins. Of course, Casey knew that there was a twin-risk, especially with the amount of money she was spending at the fertility clinic every month. Casey immediately called Steve to invite him over for dinner. After wining, dining, and sexing him, she made mention that they were going to have a baby. Steve became excited and sad all at the same time. He wanted to be a father, but he was still married to his wife. Steve was caught in a catch-22 situation. Then he asked, "How do I know it's mine?" She immediately pulled out a box of condoms that had holes in every one of them and then said, "You don't have to believe it, a paternity test will decide for us." Steve immediately got up and walked out. He did not call her for several days, but Casey was not worried. She had him by the balls and knew it. She knew that he needed her business knowledge in order to keep making money, and she knew that he was not the type of man that would put his emotions in front of the dollar sign. As Casey predicted, He was back with her spending even more time at her place. Steve had been using and mooching off women his whole life; and, when Casey finally realized that she was being used; she began to use her sex as a weapon to entrap Steve. He had no *intention of committing to Casey, much less leaving his wife; however, having kids along with the cost of child support changed things.*

Steve weighed the pros and cons while realizing the price tag associated with staying married. So, he decided to divorce his barren wife and married Casey, who was the mother of his 2 boys.

Steve and Casey are still married. However, Steve loves money, and he would dare not risk cheating on Casey for the fear of losing everything. He knows that Casey would do anything to get and keep her man.

Casey knew how to get Steve in a box, and she knew how to keep him there. Was she right about it? Absolutely not. She knew his weakness, and he gave in.

Putting people in a box is one of the quickest ways to bring about rebellion in your house, your environment, and on the job. We are designed to soar freely, so we must be able to freely give of ourselves without being forced to do so. We must also recognize the needs of others in order to better fulfill our own needs. And, for that reason, we must find a way to effectively communicate without confrontation.

Furthermore, when people feel as if they are confronted, they will rebel or shut-down and these are the two things that we must avoid at all cost. I have found that if we want to communicate with others about our wants and needs, we must find a way to speak that other person's language or we may not get in.

When we share, take action, and encourage ourselves and others, we then open up the box to allow the true essence of who we are to come out without others taking offense. We do not have to make others feel obligated to us, when they will do it naturally if we give them the room to do so. You are here to make a difference! It is through you that your spouse, mate, or partner can be reached, and it's your responsibility to make a positive impact on them, in spite of your challenges or setbacks.

39th Type of Person to Avoid

Avoid People Who Have An Ulterior Motive

When building effective relationships, negotiating with an ulterior motive is a quick way to put a ripple effect in our integrity; regardless of whether we value it or not. When we are upfront and honest about our intents, we are able to earn more respect from those who are easily scorned. When we know and understand who we are, what we want, and why we want it, we are better able to make the necessary adjustments to accommodate the situations or circumstances at hand without beguiling anyone or anything to get what we want. In my opinion, to preserve our sanity, we need to avoid those who are always trying to get us in the bed. If they are always trying to get us in the bedroom, it does not take long to figure out what the relationship is based upon. A relationship is doomed if it's just confined to the bedroom. Paul is a prime example of this:

Paul was infatuated by pretty women; all he wanted was one thing,

Chapter 5 | Ruby Fleurcius

and he did not make it a secret. His whole conversation is always about sex, so it did not take a rocket scientist to figure out what he's all about.

Paul went out to a social gathering where he met Erica, who was out looking for Mr. Right. Paul did not waste any time approaching Erica because she was quite stunning. Paul handed her his business card, and went on his way scoping out other women, giving out at least 20 business cards that night. Instead of him getting to know a woman, he would hand out business cards to rope them in, because he understood that most women are caught up in titles. It was all a game to him, so he used it as leverage to cover up his insecurities before they found out that he wasn't what he appeared to be. He firmly believed in the 80/20 rule, 80% of the women he handed his card to would never call and 20% would call back. Low and behold, Erica became that 20% who made the follow-up phone call, as she really believed that he was interested in her.

As Paul and Erica got to know each other, he made her think that he was such a wonderful man and that all he needed was a good woman. He ran the game down on Erica to get her goodies, and she gave in. She fell for the okey-doke! However, Erica soon realized that his method of operation was to play one woman against the other, making them jealous, confused, and needy. He knew that once a woman feels as if she's competing, she would give up all the goods in her candy store, without them having a clue that he did not want them.

Paul and his friends would sit around talking about the women who gave up their goodies, hoping they would be the one. They figured every woman wanted a man with a 6-figure income, and they would do anything to get him; but, Paul realized that there was something different about Erica. Erica protected her candy like it was gold; she did not care how much money he made—she was not willing to give out her treats to be tricked in the end. He would tell her about all the women, who were emotionally entangled or emotionally wounded because he decided to move on, which made Erica put locks and chains on her candy store. She felt as if Paul had no value in her, because if he did, he would never tell her about another woman.

After many moons of listening to his escapades, Erica began to feel sorry for his victims. However, she knew that she had to preserve whatever she had for her Mr. Right. And, one day he came along, she had not a clue that her Mr. Right would lavish her with the candy of his love, attention, and adoration. Michael immediately recognized that Erica was a Queen, and He had the utmost respect for her. Erica could not ask for a better man; he told her that he was going to plant a tree of love representing his love for her. He promised her that he would water that tree every day while believing that God would allow that tree to grow.

Several months later, Michael called Erica to let her know that their tree of love broke ground and that their love would never die. It seemed too good to be true, as Erica wanted to doubt his love, but Michael refused to allow her to do so. He had hope in their relationship, and he would not do anything to destroy what they have worked so hard to build. So, Erica decided that he was the one for her, and then opens her candy store of love as well. They were a match made in heaven, and he would do anything to empower her, and she would do anything to empower him.

He decided that they were going to get married and have a baby; Erica agreed to get married on one condition—her baby had to have his blue eyes. And, he agreed as long as their baby had her beautiful hair.

Chapter 5 | Ruby Fleurcius

Michael and Erica did get married. They made a joke about their baby, but he was indeed born with beautiful black hair like his mom and blue eyes like his dad. Paul eventually got married, while missing out on Erica because he played one game too many. Erica sends a message to everyone, "Protect your candy, because if you share it with everyone, what will you have left when you meet the right person?"

Even if we have been addicted to cheating, a reformed cheater, or a cheating victim, constructive knowledge that's applied in the right direction has enough strength to empower us to succeed where we have previously failed. The groundwork for greatness starts with a constructive way of thinking and living that provides a benefit to ourselves as well as the person who we are in a relationship with. When we leave ourselves unchecked and insensitive to others, we will find ourselves wearing people down that we should be building up. When we drain others, rest assured that people will soon start draining us. However, we have control over this process whether we realize it or not. If we simply choose to treat our spouse, partner, or mate really pleasant, despite what they do, say, or become, we then give our credibility enough room to create a personal magnet that has a hidden appeal of greatness. As a matter of fact, the way in which we build ourselves up or tear ourselves down on a daily basis determines the level of greatness that we will attain. As well as the amount of greatness that we bring into the lives of the people that are in our circle. In so many words, what we do with and for ourselves daily, governs our ability to become great or destructive in our relationships.

40th Type of Person to Avoid

Avoid People Who Do Not Appreciate You

The factor of appreciation has the power to take us a lot further thanbuying our way through life. How often do we show appreciation to our spouse, mate, or partner? If we really take a look within ourselves, we will find that we sometimes forget to say "Thank-you" or "I appreciate you" quite often. Furthermore, the lack of appreciation will cause the best of us to feel like a victim or feel as if we are being used; therefore, causing our natural defense system to kick into high gear. Of course, our ego contributes to some form of selfishness; however, it does not supersede the power of a simple "Thank-you" or "I appreciate you." Saying it, is just as important as showing it; regardless of whether we feel as if it is deserved or not.

Appreciation is not bought; it is given. Buying our way through life will only get us so far, especially when it comes down to the person we sleep with every night. We will never see appreciation packaged on a shelf; therefore, it's intangible! However, we are able to give something as a token of our appreciation, but when it comes down to true appreciation; we cannot put a price tag on it. When it comes down to your relationship with the one you love, let nothing take the place of a simple "Thank-you" or "I

Chapter 5 | Ruby Fleurcius

appreciate you." If you want to be appreciated, simply give appreciation with no strings attached.

41st Type of Person to Avoid

Avoid People Who Are Not Committed

Inspired commitment has more power than demanding a commitment from those who are designed to have a free-will.

A relationship that falls apart can come back together and a relationship that's together can fall apart, if we do not evaluate what we are doing or what we are not doing in our relationship. Regardless of where we may have failed, we can succeed in our relationships if we apply the simple principles that are being learned out of this book.

When building or enhancing your relationship, make sure you lay the proper groundwork to ensure that it becomes an asset and not a liability. When you are married and have sex, you become bonded: bonding of the mind (you think alike), bonding of the body (you love each other; you make love and are not just having sex), bonding of the soul (you relate to each other's emotions), and bonding of the spirit (you relate to God in the same way). In a relationship, without a commitment, bonding cannot take place, and there will be misunderstandings, frustrations, bitterness, and jealousy. I'm not saying that the bonding process will be smooth, but if you are on the same wavelength, you will be able to work problems out.

42nd Type of Person to Avoid

Avoid People Who Give Up On You

Most often, it is when we are so close to having the desires of our heart that we give up. Giving up too soon or not trying at all has and will hinder those who become stagnate in their way of thinking. When we want something out of our relationship, sitting on the couch day in and day out, is not going to get it! We must get up out of our comfort zone and do something about the situation or circumstance we are in without expecting others to do it for us.

If you are waiting for someone to believe in you or your relationship with someone, stop waiting. It starts with you believing in you. As a matter of fact, no one can truly believe in you better than you can. You have what you have—work with it. You are who you are—work with it. It is what it is—work with it. There is no need to beat yourself up about people, places, and things that you cannot change. Work with what you have to get the results that you want; and most often, your breakthrough in your relationship is usually right under your nose.

The only way to make the impossible, possible is to leave no stone unturned. We are a fountain of unlimited possibilities; therefore, we have the opportunity to exhaust all of our resources before throwing in the towel with someone or something. Giving up is easy; however, perseverance takes courage, especially when it seems as if the odds are against us. In mastering your relationships, make the impossible, possible by doing something that you have never done before and if someone gives up on you— let them go.

CHAPTER 6

Doormat of Disguise Roar

As odd as it may seem, opposite does attract; however, it's only temporary—once the newness is over or the temporary void is filled, reality will begin to set in. Once this happens, the attraction of the opposite will began to become a repellant; therefore, causing us to legitimately question our actions, thoughts, decisions, and motives. By the way, flowers, a box of chocolate, or a Teddy Bear will indeed sugar-coat this issue, but it will not fix it. Don't be fooled by going against everything you believe in—if it looks like a duck, it's a duck, and if that's not what you are looking for, don't waste your time—MOVE ON!

When you settle in a relationship, that is when you kick yourself the most, and it is also when bitterness stings the worst. The act of revenge causes you to lose value in yourself through compromising your integrity—once this is done, you will find yourself doing things that you never thought you would do. Revenge is not worth you making bad decisions or losing yourself over. Don't waste your time and energy pondering over how to bring negativity into the life of someone else. Perhaps, you may be justified in being angry; however, it does not justify wrongdoing on your part. Holding on to bitterness and resentment causes mental anguish; basically, it is a silent distraction that keeps you trapped in the past. It also drains your energy, and it puts you in a dangerous position of feeling like a victim. A victimized spirit puts your life in slow motion, and the last thing you want to do is dread living an abundant life. Inner turmoil may come, and it will go if you release the burden of carrying around the exposed bites and bruises of the past.

43rd Type of Person to Avoid

Avoid People Who Are Bitter

Instead of seeking revenge, simply allow the situation or circumstance to give you a burst of inspiration to share with others. Everything happens for a reason. Yes, it may hurt. Yes, you may want to get angry. However, saying "NO" to bitterness and resentment is worth preserving your happiness to ensure that you are able to make good, wise decisions. Easier said than done, right? Absolutely, you are going to have to push through those revengeful desires and tendencies. When you feel as if life and people have become your enemy—fight back by letting go and letting

God, which will give you the opportunity to seize the moment to be happy.

Bitterness is a byproduct of anger that's caused by disappointment or an unmet expectation. It comes into play when you allow a negative situation or circumstance to harden your heart toward someone who you felt has wronged you. Refusing to deal with your bitterness causes it to fester and grow until it consumes you, your environment, and your relationships. This is a very serious problem that will destroy you, your marriage, your children, your job, and the list goes on. Bitterness and joy cannot be felt at the same time—it's one or the other, not both. Justifying your bitterness will eventually make matters worse. When you allow bitterness to take root in your heart, it will begin to eat away at your soul, causing you to become a prisoner of your own emotions. Remember, your thoughts, actions, reactions, and feelings will govern whether your life becomes positive, productive, and fruitful. From me to you, don't let your bitterness prevent you from having what belongs to you.

44th Type of Person to Avoid

Avoid People Who Are Unforgiving

The **secret in every relationship** is to trust in God with all your heart and lean not on your own understanding—that is what gives your **relationship** its POWER. The quickest way to lose your power is through unforgiveness—it is like a ton of bricks weighing you down, draining all of your mental energy. As a matter of fact, unforgiveness is nothing more than holding a grudge; eventually, leaving you angry, bitter, and frustrated with life itself. This could possibly render you incapable of functioning normally due to the constant thoughts of getting even. Of course, no one knows what that person may have done to you, or how that person's actions may have affected you. However, you must think about what unforgiveness is doing to you right now. Don't forgive a person for their sake; forgive them for your sake. Forgiving a person will give you the freedom from inner turmoil, the freedom from bitterness, and most of all, the freedom to be YOU. An unforgiving seed that's planted in your heart will grow into a bitter and resentful tree bearing much fruit.

Many of us appearing to have it all together on the outside are afflicted with a known and unknown bitterness that's eating us up from the inside. I personally know how it feels to die a slow death from the inside out in a puddle of unforgiveness and bitterness. This is a very serious problem that will destroy you, your marriage, your children, your job, your church and the list goes on. Beware of your actions, reactions, and body language, because the fruit does not fall far from the tree. If you are harboring bitterness and resentment, it will eventually show up in some area of your life.

Forgiving is the channel through which you can release your deepest hurts and fears. Choosing to forgive does not always mean that you will forget, but it does mean that you will let go of the issue, circumstance, or situation, and never bring it up again. As a matter of fact, forgiveness is essential for your growth. Forget about your ego or pride, don't let unforgiveness rob you of your blessings. Every situation in life comes as a teacher, to give you the experience to allow you to grow and flow like never before as long as you do not allow people to push you around.

45th Type of Person to Avoid

Avoid People Who Bully You

Strife and confusion are the breeding ground for bullies, who push people around with known or unknown contention. Most often, contention goes unnoticed by the individuals who thrive off of this hidden adrenaline rush. As a matter of fact, this type of controversy provides a natural high for those who consistently take part in this type of behavior. There is no excuse for browbeating anyone.

Living a peaceful life should be one of your ultimate goals. If it is not, that's fine; but, if it is one of your goals, you must prevent strife and confusion from taking up residence in your heart. I understand that this is much easier said than done; however, you and only you have the power to overcome the negativity in your life with something positive. Bullies are not leaders, and true leaders are not bullies. Leaders exemplify their great leadership abilities by taking a negative situation and transforming it into something positive. Now, this is your opportunity to procreate harmony and allow the true essence of peace to become a representation of your inner strength.

When you remain calm and willing to listen, life will reveal hidden secrets that will propel you into your destiny. Human reasoning will fail because people and circumstances change, but the Wisdom of God does not change, and it will never fail. Wisdom is more than just common sense or knowledge; it is the ability to make godly decisions about everyday life. Knowledge can be bought, but wisdom is a gift that is used interdependently with knowledge; however, it is imperative that you do not get human reasoning confused with the Wisdom of God. It is possible to be the smartest person in the world, who have acquired an abundance of knowledge and still make unwise decisions. In my opinion, bullies are not really smart, because true wisdom would have told them that you could get more bees with honey; therefore, if you are dealing with a bully, make it your business to avoid them.

46th Type of Person to Avoid

Avoid People Who Gossip Too Much

The people, who whisper with you, will also whisper about you with or without your permission, so there is no reason to become disappointed when it happens. Who doesn't whisper? We all do at some point, some more than others; but, where do we draw the line? The line of gossiping is very thin, even for the best of us who know better. For this reason, we must make a commitment to stop becoming angry or frustrated with those who are on the gossiping end of the conversation.

Through this journey called life, I have found that it is hard to follow the story of our life when the chapters are out of order or incomplete. And, the more we try to relay our story or the stories of other people to a gossiping person, the more we become confused about the life in which we are living. Of course, we can't stop living because we fail to understand the "what's what" in our lives; however, we are able to understand that we cannot continue to fool ourselves when the "who's who" is evident. Whether we fool ourselves or not, having a Q & A session with self will definitely help us fine-tune what's up and what's not as well as who's up and who's not in our lives! If we are suffering from diarrhea of the mouth or someone we know, it is better to learn how to hold our tongue to prevent giving or receiving information that can be used against us when we least expect it.

We can boast and brag about what or who we have in our lives, but if the joke is on us, then what do we really have? Jokes are great, and you need to laugh, but I also want you to think about what and who's laughing at you. Avoid the gossiper or your life will be on BLAST!

This is definitely not what others think about you; it's about the story that YOU are creating in your own life.

When it's all said and done, what will your life tell us and who will it have made a positive impact on?

CHAPTER 7

The Uncommon Freedom Roar

Hanging on by a thread in a relationship, where you are totally dogged out, is not a great way to live. If you are totally, and I mean totally done with the relationship mentally, physically, and emotionally; and you truly want to be set free, then make a choice to move on. I know it's not always that simple, but we must find peace within ourselves somehow.

The window of opportunity will not wait for the time to be right; sometimes you just have to do it! God gave you that vision or dream to use for His Kingdom, not for it to just sit around gathering dust. Once you understand this simple fact, God will give you instructions on how to make it happen. He will provide the provisions as well as the education on how He wants the vision to fit into His Divine plan and into your destiny. Living a fulfilled life is much easier than living your life out of purpose; plus, it's better to follow the desires of your heart than to continue doing something or be around someone you hate. When you hate someone or something, it promotes other negative emotions that will eventually drive you to do things that are unwise or destructive. However, if more is desired out of life, it is mandatory to know why you do what you do and why you don't do what you need to do. Living a life full of regrets and hate is not considered to be a fulfilled life. Everything happens for a reason, and now it's up to you to live in purpose by being totally honest with yourself.

The way you think today determines what tomorrow holds for you, and what type of package it will be in. Of course, you will not be able to control everything that happens, but you can control how you deal with it. Renewing your mind on a daily basis with the Word of God, prayer, and meditation plays an important role in your destiny as well as how you will be able to deal with people. Don't forget, when laying the groundwork in a relationship, don't limit your ability to think outside, inside, around, and through the box. Here is a story that will hopefully inspire you:

Dee hired a private detective to find out if her fiancé was cheating on her. The detective then asked, "Why are you getting married, knowing that it's a possibility that he's cheating on you?" She said, "Because I have money, and He doesn't, and I am the shot-caller in this relationship!" The detective scratched his head in amazement. Even though the detective took the case; he was appalled at her attitude. Dee did a thorough background and credit check on her fiancé Malcolm to see if he was worthy of her time and effort. The detective did not catch him cheating; he had no criminal background; however, he did have a few mishaps on his credit; which Dee gave him the 3rd degree about. As a matter of fact, Dee postponed the wedding, started to date other men and refused to marry Malcolm until he was able to get his credit straight.

Malcolm was devastated; he could not believe that she could throw away true love for a credit score. He was so in love with Dee; he would worship the ground that she walked on. However, Dee kept him around as the maintenance man to fix whatever's broken; as a matter of fact, he even went a step further to keep her car clean and properly maintained. And, Malcolm gladly did so because his love was not easily turned off. Even though he was a mechanic, he did not allow his occupation to prevent him from treating Dee like a Queen. But, when Dee got around her friends, she began to treat Malcolm like a servant; she even allowed her friends to talk about him and treat him like a junkyard dog. To add insult to injury, she always appeared cold and uncaring as if he was a nobody, but when she needed something, she would always apologize and kiss up to him. However, after she got what she wanted, she was back to her old selfish ways again.

Although Dee spoke down about Malcolm being a mechanic, he allowed her criticism to inspire him to open up his own mechanic shop. After a couple of years in business, Malcolm no longer had to come home with dirt, grease, and oil under his fingernails. And, now that everything is going well for Malcolm, Dee wants to get married. On their wedding day, Malcolm finds out that Dee invited all of her ex-boyfriends to the wedding. So, instead of Dee being with her husband at their wedding, she hung out with all of her ex's, totally ignoring her husband. Dee acted as if Malcolm did not exist, this was supposed to be the happiest day of Malcolm's life and it turned out to be his worst nightmare. Malcolm's mother sobbed because she knew that her son was in love with someone who wasn't in love with him, she only married him for the money.

Malcolm grew tired and weary loving someone who did not love him. He thought that he could buy her love, but it did not work— he only bought himself more pain. He tried everything—she made it clear that she did not love him, and she could care less about the relationship. He knew that he could not live like this for the rest of his life, but he refused to allow her to make him feel as if he was worthless. Malcolm was hanging on by a thread; his heart bled constantly, as his wife openly cheated on him. So, Malcolm decides to hire an investigator, and he unknowingly hires the same investigator that his wife hired several years earlier. Amazingly, the investigator remembered this case because of Dee's arrogant attitude. As the investigator grew to know Malcolm personally, he finally told him about the statement that Dee made several years ago about her having the money and she is the shot-caller in the relationship. Malcolm could not believe she would say something of such. However, he played it cool while his investigator did his job.

One week later, the investigator catches Dee on tape with 4 different males, they all appeared to have money, they all wined and dined her, and they all had feely, touchy relationships in public. And, Malcolm remembered seeing those same 4 guys at the wedding. He was outraged, he wanted to hurt Dee; but, he could not allow Dee to turn him into someone or something that He was not raised to be. Although, he wanted to cheat and he was tempted to cheat; nevertheless, he chose to play it smart. This is what Malcolm did:

- He became 100% sure that he was done with the relationship with Dee.
- He gave himself some time to heal.
- He refused to feel like a victim.
- He began to set a guard over his heart.

Chapter 7 | Ruby Fleurcius

- He did not engage in another relationship. He had to resolve and heal from this one.
- He kept an open and guarded mind.
- He started asking questions regarding how she really felt about their relationship.
- He asked her about her expectations in the relationship. He was offended by her answers, but he kept his cool.
- He never confronted her about her infidelity. He gave her enough rope to hang herself.
- He learned how to control his emotions and act normal.
- He started paying attention to everything.
- He kept his business to himself.
- He did not indulge in any form of name-calling.
- He prepared for separation while she was out cheating and doing her thing.
- He opened a separate account and opened credit cards in his name only. (Do not empty out someone's bank account, only take what belongs to you!)
- He started looking for a place to stay.
- He made a copy of her address book, online contacts and important documents.
- He began to document everything, and he password protected it as well while taking an extra step to store it in a safe-deposit box.
- He planned for his divorce without abandoning his home.
- He got an attorney and filed for divorce.

Once the divorce papers were served, Malcolm moved out. Dee was *fine with the divorce until she realized that the men that she was cheating with were not going to do what Malcolm did; eventually, they moved on.*

Dee felt as if Malcolm would never leave because he loved her more that he loved himself. Once Malcolm started to love himself and the ground that He walked on; Dee lost her power to control, use, and abused the only true love of her life. Malcolm is now remarried with 4 beautiful children and owns a well-known full-service tire franchise. Dee lost her job, her friends, and is now working for just above minimum wage cleaning rooms just to pay off her credit card debt.

46th Type of Person to Avoid

Avoid People Who Lack Integrity

If we want to know what we think about ourselves, just look around, we are a direct reflection of what we believe. We are always on display, our thoughts are on display, our actions are on display, our reactions are on display, etc. Now, my question is, "What are you displaying right now? Do you know? Do you even care?"

When we find the common denominator of our problems, we are then better able to find a solution without losing our integrity. Whether we are on the high-end or the low-end of life, we will all have something that we need to work on. Whether it's the highest common denominator or the lowest, our best bet is to find out the what's, when's, where's, how's and why's of our problems to ensure that we do not fall by the wayside in unresolved issues or frivolous affairs. Of course, we may not have all the answers to everything in life, but we definitely have an idea regarding most things; especially, when most of our solutions are hidden deep within us.

We must take the time to evaluate what went wrong, in order to make things go right. Naturally, no one likes to be wrong, and self-correction can become difficult at times; however, when we do not know or understand the problems behind our decisions or mistakes then we subject ourselves to the aftereffect of compromise when our back is up against the wall.

The key to building strength is to keep trying, without giving up on Y.O.U. Finding the common denominator in our successes and failures in life really prepares us to go to the next level without regretting the process of doing so. Regardless of where you are in life, follow-up is key. When you master your ability to follow-up on yourself in all that you do, say and become, you will find that you are able to follow-through without losing your grip on your integrity.

47th Type of Person to Avoid

Avoid People Who Try To Block You

It is disheartening when you are doing your best, and someone comes along to block your efforts or sucker punch you. Then you ask yourself, "Why can't you get people to help you when you need it?" There are times when God blocks people from helping us in order to push us out of our comfort zone. In my opinion, it is better to adjust our thoughts and prayers to incorporate helping oneself to learn how to fish in that particular area of need, instead of being given a fish to provide temporary satisfaction. In so many words, it is better to learn how to acquire what's needed to help ourselves, opposed to being given something without learning what it takes to get it on our own. Of course, we all need a little help at some point; however, don't forget to learn the lesson that comes with learning how to fish for substance of our own to eliminate the status of codependency. Besides, depending on others to do what we are not willing to do for ourselves gives them the power to control that in which we relinquish our power to.

It is imperative that you come out of your comfort zone to think inside, outside, and around the box by learning how to fish for your own sense of uniqueness, while exhibiting your ability to become an interdependent team player that can pull your own load. Simply, take a look around you; nothing has been created on this entire earth without some type of vision.

When God created heaven and earth, He envisioned what He wanted, and it became so. We are created in His image, so what makes us any different? We have more power than we give ourselves credit for. As a matter of fact, not only do we need to have a vision of what we desire, we also need to believe in that Vision as well. I have learned throughout the years to envision what you want to become a reality, and it will be so. If someone tries to block you, go around them! When in doubt about your vision, or if you are not sure about something in your life, start writing it out to free your mind, getting your thoughts on paper. This is done by asking yourself fact-finding questions. By doing so, you will create what I call **vujá dé**, which is the opposite of déjà vu. This is where you are able to see your life from a different perspective.

When you are able to shift the perspective on your life, you are then able to shift your vision; therefore, creating a more desirable result rather than having history to repeat itself constantly, wasting precious time. If you do not shift your perspective, your life will continue the same cycle, with different scenes, characters, etc.; because if the same thing keeps happening, there is a lesson that you are not learning, and you are REQUIRED to shift your perspective to get a different result. Trust me; it's not them, it's not "IT"—it is YOU!

I must say, you are the expert in your own life, because all the answers to every problem, situation, or circumstance reside within you. However, it is hard to find the solution when you are in denial, or your mind is clouded with thoughts of too many things at once. Everyone will have some sort of fears and doubts in life. The difference is that some choose to write it out, and some choose to bounce thoughts around in their mind; eventually, becoming confused and frustrated. In order to prevent yourself from being in a state of confusion, you must release your thoughts, take your mind off of the problem, situation, or circumstance and allow the answers to flow to you naturally.

Get into the habit of putting your thoughts in writing and reviewing them periodically. When you write the final chapter of your life, what will it say? Write out what you feel inside of you, no matter how significant or insignificant it may seem for now. Whether it is a new career, getting a college degree, or losing those 20 pounds that you have been trying to lose for 10 years.

A creative idea, thought or vision that is not captured on paper is like grabbing at the wind, which could flow through your fingers at a moment's notice—some make sense, and some will not, your goal is to get it on paper. You know more about what you want than you think! Write the vision and make it plain; therefore, it makes it very easy to avoid relationships that are not conducive to the vision that's in your heart.

48th Type of Person to Avoid

Avoid People Who Do Not Believe In You

If someone does not believe in you or what you have to offer, do not waste your time trying to convince them—move on. As long as you believe in you, that's all that matters; however, you must pride yourself on your word becoming your bond. One of the greatest downfalls in a relationship is when one person stops believing in the other; and, if the believability is not restored, division takes over.

Our credibility is wrapped up in the things that we say, as well as the things that we don't say. Our lip service means nothing if action is not taking place; and, for me, the quickest way to lose credibility is to make empty promises. Believability and trust are indeed the vital ingredients that hold our credibility together, and once our credibility is ruined, it will become hard for people to trust what comes out of our mouth. Just remember, our word is our bond; therefore, we must safeguard that in which is designed to help us. In so many words, our actions must line up with what we are talking about—we can talk the talk, but if we are not walking the walk, we must question what we are speaking of. I have found that it is better to do something without saying it; than to say it, and not do it. Take a moment to line up your actions with what you are saying to ensure that your credibility does not become jeopardized by something or someone that you may have taken for granted.

Blurred images of defeat could possibly become a clear image of success in a relationship. Looking at a blurred image of something will cause your imagination to find an image that will cater to your insecurities or shortcomings. For this reason, you must understand that life does not stop to give you a moment to decide, do, or think—it continues with or without you with whatever image you hold in your mind. No matter how much success you have, if you feel defeated—life will continue to present images of defeat in your life. The best way to develop a clear image of success is to take a moment to focus on the positive, keeping an open, guarded, and non-judgmental mind about everything. By doing so, it will enable you to become stronger and wiser with every positive or negative experience. Victory starts in your mind—here are 4 clues to help clear up your vision:

- Take a look at your weak spots or your handicaps and make them your best assets instead of weaknesses. Remember, there is something positive in every situation, it's up to you to create a win-win situation by creating **vujá dé**. Shift your perspective!
- Find out what produces outstanding results for you. You don't have to understand it, in order to use it—everything will work itself out.
- Can you use it to benefit the lives of others?
- Is it worth taking the time to triumph over your tragedy?

Now, as you prepare for your destiny, focus on the little things you take for granted. Most often, your blessing will be right under your nose—wrapped in a small package.

Chapter 7 | Ruby Fleurcius

49th Type of Person to Avoid

Avoid People Who Are Deceptive

How do we know if our heart is in the right place? The best way to evaluate whether or not our heart is in the right place is to check our motives. Our motives will reveal what the heart conceals—although, we play cat and mouse games when it comes down to being true to thyself; however, our actions, reactions, and what comes out of our mouth will reveal the contents of our heart in due time. What I have found is that when we are faced with a challenging battle of the heart, it is imperative that we sit down and make a list of the pros and cons regarding our motives. This will help draw out any form of deception—plus, if we lie to ourselves, who are we really cheating? If we are doing anything out of jealousy, envy, strife, greed, revenge, anger, unforgiveness, or spite, that's an automatic sign that our heart is in the wrong place; and, we need to take it to God in prayer.

Doing the right thing for the wrong reason is just as bad as doing the wrong thing for the right reason—we need to bring our heart and mind into a positive balance with each other to prevent bad karma from showing up when we least expect it. When our heart is in the right place, it gives us confidence in knowing who we are and what we stand for. Does this mean that we are perfect? Absolutely not, we are all a work in progress, but when we have a good heart, integrity is made evident in all that we do, say, and become. I will release a little secret, when we are able to govern our heart, which means to become a good steward over our heart, we are better able to control self.

Self-control has a lot to do with the heart of man, and if we are able to understand how the two work hand-in-hand, we can become a master over our Mind, Body, Soul, and Spirit. If one has the desire for WISDOM, I am giving them the hidden secrets on a silver platter—this is indeed how I have received the wisdom that I possess today. By the way, let me drop another nugget of wisdom, we have a smorgasbord of wisdom buried within us that will flow from the depths of our soul if we do not allow folly to block our mental, emotional, or spiritual gateways. The Wisdom of God has by far trumped anything that my mind can conceive—He is always blessing me to be a blessing to others, and He will do the same for you as well. Therefore, work on getting your heart in the right place, and watch how God supernaturally pump wisdom through your veins when you least expect it.

Chapter 7 | Ruby Fleurcius

CHAPTER 8

The Roaring Mind Germ

Is it possible that our attitude, our actions, or our behavior on the outside of our house affect what takes place on the inside of our house? The answer is a quick YES for me. The Law of Reciprocity is in high effect, do not think for a minute that we can behave badly and expect peace as a result—that's not going to happen. When chaos and confusion are running rampant, we must find peace in the midst of it; according to scripture, *"He that hath no rule over his own spirit is like a city that is broken down, and without walls."* Proverbs 25:28. We cannot allow the things that are taking place around us to cause us to lose our temper or lack the self-control needed to think rationally. In my opinion, we have a lot more at stake; therefore, we must think wisely before reacting because it may affect the innocent people that we love or affect the innocent people that we know nothing about. As we all are aware that anything can happen at any given moment; therefore, we must keep our wits about us at all times.

However, I will say this; violence is not the answer! According to Proverbs 16:29, *"Violent people deceive their friends and lead them to disaster."* And, if we do not become mentally and emotionally strong about the things that are taking place around us, we will become consumed with the perplexities that are trying to keep us bound. Remember, there is nothing new under the sun, and it's through wisdom that our house is built; and it's through love, joy, peace, kindness, goodness, faithfulness, gentleness, and self-control that it is established. This will keep the **MIND CONTROL GERM** from turning one person against another to create division among us.

"He that is slow to anger *is* better than the mighty, and he that ruleth his spirit than he that taketh a city." Proverbs 16:32. Your strength and peace reside in loving and respecting all humanity regardless of creed or deed; because if you do not, true value cannot be found in the people, places, and things you hate. Exhibiting hatefulness in your actions, reactions, or spoken words will cause the true essence of a peaceful life to elude the place in which hate resides; therefore, love thy neighbor as you love thyself.

50th Type of Person to Avoid

Avoid People Who Try To Sidetrack You

Life may not be fair, but it does offer you a special gift called FAVOR if you do not allow yourself to become sidetracked by a relationship or the issues of life.

As life presents itself in many different facets, things may or may not go the way you have desired for them to go. It's possible that you may win, or you may lose at times, but with divine favor, you will lose to win and win to lose. This is the cycle of life that produces the pruning process that will eliminate the things that are not conducive to you or your well-being. As you very well know, favor may not be fair, but it does take care of the individuals who believe that they are covered with favor. If you have not noticed, favor will always prevail and work in the lives of those who make it their business to do the right thing. Opportunity and favor go hand in hand—if you want favor, embrace opportunity and if you want opportunity, embrace favor. By embracing this concept, you will be able to prosper in any given situation or circumstance regardless of the odds. Hint, hint, a tremendous amount of favor comes when you are able to take the negativity in your life and turn it into something positive.

Regardless of how much you know or don't know, life is designed to give you back what you put into it. Most often, we spend many years finding fault in ourselves, when we should be spending our time enjoying a purposeful life. In order to be more, see more, do more and have more, you must understand that you are blessed to do what you do! Are the little blessings not as important as the big ones? Little blessings and big blessings carry the same amount of weight when it comes down to the acknowledgment of what it is. There are times when we totally forget about the little blessings that take place on a daily basis—not realizing that the little blessings prepare the way for the big ones. Most often, we miss out on our blessings because we don't expect them. The key word here is expectation. Expectancy has enough power to create a day of total bliss or put a damper on the brightest man's day. Regardless of how big or small, our blessing is—if it is not recognized, it will have no apparent value. As a matter of fact, we are just as responsible for receiving our blessing as we are for **not** getting one; therefore, it is imperative that we become open and ready to giving as well as receiving.

If you have not noticed by now, anything worth having will take quite a bit of self-control, patience, discipline, determination, and most of all, persistence and commitment. Yes, it may get a little uncomfortable, but true achievement comes about when you step outside of your comfort zone into the unknown. Aiming high will produce a spark of understanding that will take you where insecurity NEVER will. Understanding can be a lot of things, but it is not rationalizing or judging. As a matter of fact, it is having the patience to see beyond your own point of view. This is not about being right or wrong; it's about being understood in a neutral environment. Understanding others as well as yourself is obligatory in breaking down the walls of inferiority. It really allows a person to feel free of all fears and limitations—which is basically the ultimate goal.

Your instincts will tell you what most people will not, the only requirement that's needed is for you to open up and listen to the voice from within. Once you are open to listening, the voice from within will speak louder than the loudest person you know. Not only that, it will give you a little nudge or a funny, uncomfortable feeling as well. This is

Chapter 8 | Ruby Fleurcius

basically your senses alerting you to pay close attention to what you are doing, what you are saying, or any decisions that you are about to make. This next story is a great example of how to avoid being sidetracked in a relationship:

God has a special veil over a few people in life, which Lisa happens to be one of them. Lisa has always been a person who knew that God had a greater purpose in her life, and for that reason, she pretty much became a loner; but for some odd reason, Lisa like going to yard sales to find hidden treasures. One Saturday, she went to a huge yard sale, and she ran into an older gentleman that was so helpful. They got to talking, not realizing that they had so much in common. Actually, Keith had known Lisa since she was a little girl; he would hang out with her father. Lisa thought it was a coincidence, but Keith had targeted Lisa for many years waiting for the right opportunity to get close to her.

Lisa's father died at a very young age, so she really missed having a father figure in her life. As Keith became so helpful, he filled a small void that Lisa wouldn't tell anyone about. And, being that Keith knew her father, she let her guards down. She looked at Keith as a 2nd father, while Keith looked at her as easy prey. He did not know that she was deeply rooted in a spiritual relationship with her Heavenly Father. Over the next several months, Lisa noticed that Keith started to become a little distant, she could not figure out what was wrong with him. So, she stopped by his house to make sure that he was okay; when she got there, he warmly greeted her and kissed her in the mouth. Lisa was grossed out, but she played it off. She could not believe he was trying to capitalize on her kindness. However, she then realized that he wanted more than a friendship, he wanted intimacy; therefore, she made it clear that he is not what she was looking for, and that she was waiting for God to send her a husband. He then proclaimed that God sent him to her, but she did not buy it. She and God had a personal relationship, and she firmly believed that if he was the right man, God would have told her so.

This proclamation of being Mr. Right went on for 6 months while Lisa became even more adamant about standing her grounds with him. Lisa felt that she had sacrificed many years of devotion to God; therefore, no one could easily convince her to enter into a relationship when her heart wasn't in it. She did not want to be deceived, and she was hell-bent on not deceiving others. Although Keith became a really good friend to her, she was not willing to risk hurting him when God had promised her a certain type of man.

After Keith had realized that his charm was not going to work, he changed his approach. He became a ruthless, conniving, and manipulative old man. Lisa never experienced a wolf in sheep's clothing, so she began to feel victimized by the way in which he tried to break her down. He tried to label her as a gold-digger, which did not work because he willfully helped her without her having to ask. He tried to label her as a whore; it did not work. He tried to make her jealous; it did not work. He actually asked her, "How can your God leave you here by yourself without a mother, father, or anyone to love, what kind of God do you serve?" After that comment, Lisa bent, but she did not break; but, she did say, "One day her God would bless her with a man beyond her wildest dreams." Keith broke her heart, but she refused to allow him to break her spirit. It was definitely time for Lisa to move on with her life and to live her life the way God intended.

Lisa's relationship with God has indeed blessed her with a great husband, who has everything she wants or needs in a man, and she did not have to commit fornication to get him.

She and her husband went on to build a well-known multi-million dollar empire. Keith is now unhappily married and broke; however, Lisa and her husband send him a monthly allowance check that's labeled, "A gift from God." Her husband was so glad that she waited patiently on him; Lisa was everything that he prayed for in a woman.

51st Type of Person to Avoid

Avoid People Who Try To Get In Your Head

How do we keep our composure when someone is trying to get in our head? In order to keep our composure, we must develop and nurture the control of self. In my opinion, everyone thinks that they have self-control, and they are correct to a certain extent; however, if the actions, reactions, and the attitude of what we consider being our form of self-control are bringing about negativity, violating the will of others, or causing harm to ourselves or others, one must wonder is it really **SELF** that has control over us.

Our behavior and what comes out of our mouth reveals the contents of our heart, regardless of how hard we try to cover it up; therefore, giving birth to self-deception, allowing us to criticize or belittle others for the same things that we are guilty of. If this type of deception is not corrected, we unawaringly cause certain behaviors, practices, or characteristics to hover over our home to affect the weakest link, and most often, it is our children. If we look around, we will find that we must take a different approach to understanding and change our behavior, attitude, and mindset that are focused inwardly first, and then permeating as a ray of love, hope, and peace outwardly.

Once we can do that, then the Power of Prayer will make the appropriate corrections necessary with the people, places, and things we come in contact with on a daily basis. When we activate and understand self-control with the foundation of prayer, we have a little more stability to walk in faith with what we believe, not just by what we are taught or conditioned to think. The Power of our Instincts are attached to the Power of our Self-Control, and they will both grant us wisdom; however, if we want one without the other, we will find that they will cause a spiritual imbalance within the depths of our soul due to the lack of understanding between the two. How do we get the two to meet up? Great question! I am going to reveal another **Spiritual Secret**—the way in which to get our self-control to meet up with our instincts; we must **FAST**.

The Power of Fasting is the **ONLY** way to make our instincts meet up with our self-control, chasing the spirit of deception out of our loins to make the appropriate spiritual connections. "But I keep under my body, and bring it into subjection: lest that by any means, when I have preached to others, I myself should be a castaway. 1 Corinthians 9:27. Because, as Jesus clearly states in Mark 9:29, "This kind can come forth by nothing, but by prayer and fasting." If no one tells us, I will say it! **FASTING** has more power than we care to imagine as long as we do not use it to violate the will of another person. When we use it to empower ourselves, we gain the power over our flesh, we gain the power over our mind, we gain the power over our emotions, we gain the power over out of control situations, circumstances, and events that are beyond our control, and it gives us the power to rout demons in spiritual warfare.

Our faith is under attack, and if we do not get a grip and clear up this misunderstanding, we are going to become consumed by this **MIND CONTROL GERM** that has been planted in our community to break us as a nation. We do not need more violence; we need more people who are willing to **FAST** this nation through these atrocities to put self-control back into its proper perspective. In creating the appropriate circles, I need you to do your part in sowing love, joy, peace, kindness, goodness, faithfulness, gentleness, self-control, fasting, and spreading this word of hope.

52nd Type of Person to Avoid

Avoid People Who Wage Spiritual Warfare Against You

Is spiritual warfare real? Absolutely! Spiritual warfare is all around us, and it has been since Adam and Eve—it has been battling for its territory, and it's not going anywhere. In my opinion, spiritual warfare is real, and it can become very dangerous if we are not prepared for it or uninformed about it. Most often, we have been conditioned to think that spiritual warfare is not real or that it simply does not exist, but if we look around to see what is taking place right now, we will understand that this is not about us, it is a spiritual battle that's bigger than us. According to Ephesians 6:12, *"For we wrestle not against flesh and blood, but against principalities, against powers, against the rulers of the darkness of this world, against spiritual wickedness in high places."* It is a battle that's destroying families, it's a battle that's destroying faith, it's a battle that's destroying hope, and it's a battle that's destroying our ability to trust in those who are designed to serve and protect. This type of mental or emotional enslavement should not exist, but it does! We are living in fear in the land of the FREE! We are allowing it into our homes, churches, workplaces, communities, etc. Although, some of this MIND CONTROL GERM phenomenon is being forced upon us; however, we must become mentally, emotionally, physically, and spiritually strong to endure this type of warfare. This is a STRONGHOLD that has us bound right now, we must recognize it for what it is—until then, we are going to become a laughing stock for all onlookers to see that we are not so free after all if we are bound mentally. We are not just fighting for the peace in our homes, we are fighting for our loved ones, we are fighting for the peace of our nation, and we are fighting for the Kingdom of God. Once we recognize this battle for what it is, we are better able to become equipped for it—as I said previously, violence is not the answer—PRAYER is. Remember, this is a God ruled nation, and if we are trusting a man to fix this issue, our trust is indeed in the wrong place. The Book of Proverbs in the Bible tells us more about Godly character that will keep our families and our Nation together, but it is overlooked, then we wonder why social media has taken over.

Pray over your loved ones before they leave home, pray for them when they get back, pray for them before they go to sleep at night, keep yourself prayed up, and pray for everyone. God's grace and mercy are real, He is no respecter of persons, He reigns on the just and the unjust alike; and, He loves us all no matter what! Fast and pray for the Land of the FREE, your mental, physical, emotional, and spiritual freedom depends on it!

CHAPTER 9

The Roaring Cheater from Within

Who likes to be cheated on? Absolutely no one, right? Cheating is all around us, as it is also within us. We can't get away from it, unless we are truly able to understand it. I could very well say avoid a cheater, but I cannot say that! As we all know, cheating has contributed to more broken relationships than we care to imagine; however, cheating can also cause us to recognize where we are falling short as well. In order to truly understand the profile of a cheater, we must understand that there are multiple ways of cheating. Of course, we are all familiar with cheating physically, but what about cheating emotionally, mentally, or spiritually? We do not talk about the other ways of cheating, nor do we talk about the way we cheat ourselves. Now the question is, "Can we really cheat on ourselves?" Absolutely. We cheat ourselves all the time without giving it a second thought.

Once we truly understand the meaning of cheating, we are better able to understand our relationships, the relationships of others, and the reality of what's not being said. This hush, hush mentality has broken up more homes than we care to imagine; and, for some odd reason, we as a society could care less about fixing the issue.

I understand quite well that it's odd or uncomfortable to be labeled as a cheater or cheatee; however, in order to understand the person who has cheated on you, you must understand the cheater that's within your very own soul. Regardless of whether you are single, married, divorced, or anywhere in between, this book will help you deal with the untold issues that take place in our homes that we cannot tell anyone about. Yes, these are our deepest, darkest secrets that we most likely would take to our grave, before we would risk becoming embarrassed about exposing how we really feel, or what's really taking place behind closed doors. Of course, this book will not full-proof you or your relationships; but, it will definitely prepare you on how to deal with, sift through, overlook or get rid of the people you don't want to ensure that you attract what you do want. This book is not designed to break-up relationships; it's designed to restore that in which is destined to be. So, today is your day to stop wasting your time on dead-end relationships that are constantly causing you some sort of unwanted or unjust pain.

Although we all like to play around with words, and we are accustomed to softening up words to make them appear appealing to certain classes of people. And, I am guilty of doing such myself—I play with words quite often; and, I was approached with this question some time ago, "Once a cheater, always a cheater?" I tried to soften it up as much as possible, but the look on my face told the absolute truth.

Chapter 9 | *Ruby Fleurcius*

Then the person asked me the question again by rephrasing the question with a "yes" or "no" answer. Well, it took me a minute, I looked down—I paused for a brief second and honestly answered the question with tears in my eyes. My answer was "YES." I knew that answering that question honestly would carry a lot of heat for me; but, in all honesty—I did not care. The truth of the matter is according to scripture; there is temptation in every man, and there is temptation in every woman—look at Eve!

If you are not God—then every woman or man has his or her price given the right situation, circumstance, event, or trauma. In my opinion, it is only God that keeps us from falling into diverse temptation; and, if we do not depend on Him for certain things, we do not know what we would do in certain situations, events, or circumstances. I have found when a woman or man is hurt, they have done the unthinkable—the prison system is a prime example, one mistake is all it takes. Not only that, we have all made mistakes that we are not proud of, that we would never tell anyone about—yet, we still pass judgment on those who are making the same mistakes. That is the very reason why I answer that question honestly because I knew that I would get a little heat behind it, and I would have to write a book to enlighten the naysayers on how easy it is for Mr. or Mrs. Faithful to become Mr. or Mrs. Cheater.

We all have a cheater inside of us, whether you are with the right or the wrong person. The spirit of cheating is directly linked to our human nature, which can very well be controlled like any other habit or addiction. Just because we are created a certain way does not mean that we should lack self-control. There are consequences and repercussions behind the known or unknown choices that we make. Of course, we all want to play a little naive from time-to-time, pretending that everyone is faithful when our divorce rate is at its highest. As a matter of fact, infidelity has a way of creating a breeding ground of broken trust, betrayal, and insecurity without us realizing what's really happening.

Cheating can be formed out of a habit, addiction, conditioning, revenge, need, or greed! However, we will always have the option to cheat or **not** to cheat, which reflects our power of choice. I must add, if we give in to cheating, the urge will only grow stronger if we do not recognize the underlying source or seed. Can a cheater stop cheating? The answer is "NO." As I said earlier, there is a cheater inside every one of us; however, a cheater can change his or her ways that will prevent the act of cheating. An individual who enjoys cheating must find a way not to put himself or herself in the position to become tempted. This must be CONTROLLED! Temptation has a way of causing the best of us to fall short when we take our eyes off of our human nature. Can anything good come of this? Absolutely, if the desire for change outweighs their desire to cheat. However, the temptation to cheat will never go away; but the desire to cheat can be repressed or suppressed out of the fear of loss. For example, if you fear losing your wife or husband, then more than likely you will put the act of cheating under subjection; but, if there is not a fear of loss, then cheating could become open gain for all of those who may fall victim to the pain of cheating.

Even though we may feel as if we have gotten away

with the act of cheating, we have not. The act of cheating and deception keeps us confused and unsatisfied while opening the door to more undue stress and loss. When we judge others for cheating, we unknowingly ignite the same desire within our very own soul. Although we do not admit this, the proof is in our divorce rate. Even though we may not commit the physical act of cheating, we commit the mental or emotional acts of cheating to hurt those who may have hurt us. For the record, there are 5 types of cheating:

1. Physical Cheating
2. Emotional Cheating
3. Mental Cheating
4. Spiritual Cheating
5. Cyber Cheating

Most often, we are quick to judge those who are caught in the act of adultery or those who are caught simply cheating. But, how do we explain our acts of emotional cheating? Okay, what's emotional cheating? Emotional cheating is when we engage in having an emotional bond or when we depend on some form of emotional support from someone outside of our primary relationship. We will find that these types of affairs provide a safety net or comfort zone that cannot be experienced at home; therefore, causing constant comparison or dissatisfaction in the primary relationship.

53rd Type of Person to Avoid

Avoid People Who Deprive You Emotionally

Emotional deprivation or emotional affairs have caused just as many break-ups as the physical act of cheating. We are emotional beings, and when we become starved emotionally, it creates a void that's easily replaced with physical infidelity; but not limited to. I have found that emotional cheating is on the rise thanks to the wonderful thing called the internet.

The internet has provided a gateway to emotional cheating, more so than physical cheating itself. As a matter of fact, let's talk numbers, 44% of married men have been unfaithful, 36% of married women have been unfaithful at some point in their marriage, 66% of those who are married engage in online adultery or affairs, and 83% of married couples have considered committing adultery—those numbers are ridiculous! So who is lying to whom? We dare not tell anyone our innermost thoughts; we can fool everyone else, but I am not the one to fool. We are created to love and be loved; if we are missing the emotional bonding or mental bonding process, we will fill in the gap somehow, and cyber cheating is on the rise!

Emotional cheating is a hidden vice of those who are in denial of their longing for more than what they have. As I watch social media expand, I am amazed at how many people neglect their wives or husbands to develop new friends, new contacts, while chatting for hours feeding their emotional hunger. Of course, social media is wonderful, and it's a great networking tool, but it also opens the door to cheating on a more sophisticated level.

Now the question is, "Can you really love someone you don't know or have never seen?" Although some would say yes, my answer is "NO!" In my opinion, when dealing with relationships, we must bond mentally, physically, emotionally and spiritually—if we have not come into physical contact with a person, we are going to miss something. We can certainly care about someone, as well as his or her well-being, or maybe even to fill a temporary void; nevertheless, love is a little different. I have found that most often we confused love with infatuation because we allow our feelings to override our sense of good judgment. When we cannot see, feel, or touch someone, our mind will create an image of what we desire; and, most often our desires are centered around power, money, and sex.

It is our mental perception that causes our mind to create a mental picture of superficial love; and, once we remove those elements of power, money, and sex out of the equation, we will find that the conditions of our infatuation will change quickly. If left unchecked, our infatuation will turn into resentment, hate, or repulsiveness when we are rubbed the wrong way. Now, on the other hand, real love is unconditional—if we are able to be around someone without power/status/fame, without having a dime in their pocket, without having sex with them, we will find that we will begin to have a longer lasting relationship of substance that will turn into love. I am not saying that we must become blinded by love, or to settle for less, all I am saying is to be true to thyself about who and what we love without allowing our infatuation to place us in a position that will compromise our integrity or our purpose.

When we are able to truly love ourselves first, we are better able to love and let go, exercise tough love, love freely, or place limits on what may cause a derailment in our lives. Furthermore, if an unconditional friendship is not developed before the infatuation wears off, it's possible that the relationship will soon feel like a prison sentence; especially, when dealing with this new wave of cyber love, cyber cheating, and cyber sexting. Therefore, it is best to make sure that infatuation is not getting the best of you—plus, if you have not experienced at least 4 seasons with someone to feel the ups and downs in a relationship, BEWARE! With every season change will come—if you have not been through the seasons together, you can rest assured once the newness wears off, your eyes will be opened to reality! Check out this story:

"Lloyd has a great marriage, and he loved socializing and hung out with his family. At Lloyd's annual company meeting, he received a bonus check for a substantial amount. He and his wife agreed that he should spend a portion of his money to get a new laptop for himself. Lloyd became so excited about not sharing a computer with his kids that he ordered his computer right away. When Lloyd received his computer from Dell, he was so happy that he spends the entire weekend playing with his new boy-toy. His wife did not mind, she and the boys had a great weekend without him anyway.

Over the next several months, Lloyd became very distant. He no longer had an interest in his wife, his kids, or any family activities. Lloyd's wife grew extremely concerned about him because:

- *His sleep pattern changed, he no longer wanted to go to bed at a reasonable time.*
- *He ate dinner at his computer.*
- *He became extremely protective over his computer.*
- *He demanded his privacy when he was on the computer.*
- *He made the boys do his household chores.*
- *He started to become a different person.*
- *He had no desire for sex.*
- *He began to lie about what he was doing on the computer.*
- *He gave up watching his favorite television shows.*
- *He began to hide his laptop.*

Lloyd's wife started feeling lonely, confused, rejected, and abandoned. She felt as if she was to blame, so she asked him if he was cheating on her and he answered "no" and went back to the computer. She could not believe that she was so easily replaced by a computer. Lloyd saw that his wife really needed his attention, so he cut back on his computer activity. And, even though he cut back on his computer activity, Lloyd enjoyed and became addicted to having an online rendezvous with different people and has no intent to stop."

Lloyd is still married and is comfortable with having Cyber Affairs. He does not consider it cheating, so he continues to do so while putting his family on a schedule. He plans how much time that he's going to spend with his wife, his kids, with the family as a whole, and with his Cyber Mistresses. His wife has accepted the fact that he's addicted to the internet, and as long as she gets her time, she's okay.

When we depend on someone other than our spouse or mate for emotional support, relief or comfort, we must exercise extreme caution. It is easy to become emotionally bonded to someone that you communicate with more than your spouse, whether it is male or female. For example, when you become excited to hear from someone or depend on hearing from someone that's not your spouse or your mate, this should be a red flag. Having a friend that's easy to talk to is great, but if you are more comfortable talking to them rather than your spouse, something is wrong!

54th Type of Person to Avoid

Avoid People Who Deprive You Sexually

Most often men cheat because they are deprived sexually and women cheat because they are deprived emotionally. So, what do we have here? I will tell you; it's a disaster waiting to happen. When we feel underappreciated, whether it's a male or female, the cheater from within will try to gain access to our outer world. Regardless of whether or not the capacity to cheat is acted upon or not, we are still human, and we need to understand the underlying reason for the provocation of the cheater from within.

Some people are addicted to cheating, and there is nothing that we can do about it but to accept it or not to accept it. We are accustomed to hearing about alcohol, drug, smoking, or food addictions, but for some reason, we overlook those who are addicted to cheating. As a matter of fact, cheating addictions are not really recognized at all by today's society. We just label them as a player or whore, and call it a day. As a result, it has created a domino effect of unhealthy, unsafe, and dysfunctional relationships that keeps the cycle going. For those who are addicted to cheating will often get an adrenaline rush by having an emotional, physical, mental, or cyber affair with someone other than their spouse. This type of excitement can easily become a silent addiction to the effects that cheating provokes. For example, some cheaters are addicted to the act of betrayal, some are addicted to deception, some are addicted to lying, some are addicted to the drama, some are addicted to the spying, some are addicted to conquering the hard-to-get people, and some are addicted to the breakup or the make-up process. Who knows; but what I do know, is that a person who's addicted to cheating gets bored really quick. However, they very well may have a primary relationship that they will protect at all cost, or they may have that primary relationship to spark the drama. It really depends on the psychological needs of an addicted cheater, which leads us to our next story about Monica:

Monica met her boyfriend through a mutual friend, although he was a tad bit older, she fell in love with him. Her boyfriend, Mike, knew that she was a good girl, so he never wanted her to know that he was addicted to cheating. Monica trusted Mike with all her heart; she never questioned him about anything, because he never gave her a reason to distrust him. As time passed in the relationship, they knew that they were meant to be together. They were inseparable, and everyone knew this. She would allow her friends to come over and hang out without giving it a second thought.

Monica and her best friend, Jada went on a road trip, touring many different places in St. Louis. They had such a wonderful time; Jada decided to stay another week. Monica had to work, so she left Jada with Mike. He would take her everywhere she needed to go, and they had a great time. All of a sudden, Mike seduced Jada. Jada gave in, and they continue their affair for her entire stay while Monica was at work. Monica did not have a clue; she would never think that Mike would sleep with another woman; especially not her best friend. However, Monica did notice that Jada acted a little strange when Mike catered to her, but she just blew it off.

After Jada had left to go back home, Mike began to label Jada as a whore—which was very strange; especially, after he was so nice to her. Several months thereafter, Jada calls to warn Monica to watch her man. Of course, Monica gets curious and questions why Jada would say anything of such. Nevertheless, Monica starts to pay attention to Mike's actions. One day she came home from work early and caught Mike with another woman in their house. Monica was devastated, she went crazy; she could not believe her eyes. Mike was shocked that Monica caught him cheating; he tried to lie his way out of it, but the cat was out of the bag.

Monica called Jada to tell her what happened, as Monica dialed the number, she had a premonition of Mike and Jada in her bed. So, instead of telling Jada what happened, she told Jada that she was not upset with her, but she needed to ask a very important question. As Jada became a little nervous, she said, "Okay." Monica then asked, "Did Mike do anything to you when you were here." She responded, "What do you mean." Then Monica rephrased the question, "Did you and Mike sleep together while you were here." She paused and *then answered, "Yes." Jada began to tell Monica every detail about what happened, she even told her about his distinctive birthmark. She said that she was afraid to say anything.*

Mike was Monica's first real boyfriend, so it took some time for her to get over him cheating. So, Monica began to probe for answers and what she found out was astounding. Mike had slept with 5 more of her friends, her cousin, and her sister. Monica was so ashamed of Mike's behavior; she broke up with Mike vowing never to go back to him. And, she still hasn't healed totally due to the profound embarrassment that she allowed him to take her through.

Monica has moved on with her life and is doing quite well without Mike. She still believes that Mike was her soul mate, but she was not able to live with the damage that Mike unjustly inflicted upon her. Monica is a God-fearing woman who believes in second chances, and she believes that God has given her a second chance to find the mate of her soul. Mike hasn't changed, he presently has 4 different girlfriends and still searching for the love that Monica once shared with him.

55th Type of Person to Avoid

Avoid People Who Exhibit Foolish Behavior

How can we recognize foolishness? We have all done something that we are not proud of, and we will all fall short at some point in our lives. However, if we are always falling short or if we are always doing things that we are not proud of, then it is fair to say that is indeed recognition of foolish behavior.

When we are doing things that will affect us, our family, or the innocent negatively or out of selfishness, we must question our reasons for such folly. The Bible speaks of foolishness, folly, and waywardness time and time again; yet we continue to exhibit selfish behaviors to quench an inner thirst from within, not realizing that we will thirst again. The more we partake of foolishness, the more we will crave it; and, the more we crave it, the more we become engulfed in that type of behavior causing our conscience to take a back seat. In my opinion, an idle mind becomes the Devil's playground to overthink and create issues that are only real to the person that's allowing him to play! Once this happens, we can bank on folly seeping out of our loins even if we think that we are right in our own eyes.

How do we know if it's happening to us? Mental exhaustion is the first sign, feeling stressed out is the second sign, and feeling depressed is the third sign—this type of violation will breakthrough when we are mentally, emotionally, physically, and spiritually weak. The best way to safeguard our mind or shut down the Devil's playground is to stay busy, pray, read the Bible, know how to apply the Scriptures to practical life, and create a win-win situation out of everything.

When our muscles are tense, so is our brain; therefore, breaking our flow. Once our flow is broken, we will find that everything will begin to hit us at once to shift our state of being. If we have a desire to maximize our full potential, we must give our bodies the opportunity to relax first, and then allow it to perform mentally, emotionally, physically, or spiritually. I am living proof, when we respect our bodies, it will respect us. This is your opportunity to shut down the Devil's playground mentally, emotionally, physically, and spiritually to safeguard your ability to think clearly, relax, and allow your creative juices to flow; therefore, creating a win-win situation out of yesterday's mistakes.

CHAPTER 10

The Right A Wrong Roar

In today's time, with the fast movement of social media, we can become known for what we want to be known for; however, once our credibility is lost, it is hard to regain. For most, we have learned that a good name is chosen; and, what we do not realize is that our integrity, credibility, and character are a part of our name. Yes, it comes as a package deal; and once it is gone, sugar-coating it will not work.

Who cares about a name, integrity, or credibility as long as we are getting what we want, right? Wrong, whether we are at the top or the bottom of the ladder of success, we need to exercise caution when sugar-coating our reality. If we lose our integrity or credibility, what's the probability of having a good name or reputation? We all know that it is highly improbable, if we don't know—it is fair to say that we are in denial. In my opinion, people will remember a negative past before they will acknowledge a positive future, because hurt will weaken the heart, rejection will weaken the heart, loss will weaken the heart, lack of support will weaken the heart, etc. Regardless of how we try to right a wrong, people will remember how we disappointed them or how we made them feel, first. Even though we may feel that this is our life, we can live it how we want, and run the race that we so desire; however, we must understand that we are not in this world alone. The rat-race of real life does not tolerate bad karma— what we give out, will come back to us; that is indeed the Law of the Land.

Your credibility and integrity are characteristics that you do not want to lose. And, if you have lost or tarnished it, let no one take the love that you have for life away from you or prevent you from doing what's in your heart. Furthermore, when it comes down to the matters of the heart, there is nothing wrong with running your own race, just choose your race carefully as you make the necessary changes to take yourself to the next level.

56th Type of Person to Avoid

Avoid People Who Are Envious OR Jealous Of You

How do we deal with people who do not like us? If someone does not like us, that is their problem, not ours, unless we have given them a reason to dislike us. If

Chapter 10 | Ruby Fleurcius

someone does not get to know the true person that we are, then it's time to move on anyway. If we are doing the right thing by operating in outright integrity, we do not need to convince a person to like us, nor do we have to change who we are to fit into a particular circle just to become likable.

It is imperative that we come into our own individuality; as long as we are not operating in waywardness to cause people to dislike us, then we have nothing to worry about. In my opinion, it is only envy, jealousy, or hatefulness that would cause one to dislike those who they know nothing about. However, if we are exhibiting negative characteristics to offend, betray, or hurt innocent people, then one should have the option to dislike our behavior, attitude, action, or reaction. It does not matter what we do, say, or become, someone is not going to like it, or someone may have something to say about it, but we cannot allow it to stop us from becoming who God created us to be.

Our value does not reside in someone liking us; our value resides in us liking ourselves for who we are. When we lose value in ourselves, we will depend on others to value us instead; and, when that does not happen, we will feel as if we are unworthy of his or her love. In my opinion, that should not be the case, but it happens all too often. How do we know if we are valuable to someone? We will know if someone values us when we find value in ourselves first. If we do not find value in ourselves, we will not appreciate the fact that a person has found us to be valuable; therefore, we will become ungrateful, taking more than we are giving. This is exactly how people tend to get used and abused because most often people will treat us based on how we see and treat ourselves, unless they are being vindictive; trying to break down a person who takes pride in themselves. Nevertheless, we can spot those types of individuals by where they place their value; as a rule of thumb, what we find value in gets our love, time, money, priority, and other resources.

If we pay closer attention to this, it will indeed safeguard one from a lot of deceptive people. What we value enables us to set priorities of what's important to us; but when our values are not in the right place, we will find that we will begin to make bad decisions, wrong decisions, or controlling decisions based upon where our heart is. Listen, where there is no value found in what we have to offer, we must find a way to get into an environment where our true value is found. In so many words, deal with people that bring out the best and not the worst—when we become better, and not bitter about how we live our lives, as well as how we see ourselves, our whole outlook on life will change. Knowing your values enable you to set priorities of what's important to you; it will also help you get rid of the people, places, and things that are not conducive to where you are going as well.

This brings me back to a pivotal moment that I will never forget as long as I live: After recovering from a minor stroke, I had a few setbacks health-wise; however; I was invited to an event, and upon leaving I decided to take a plate to go. This particular individual intentionally tried to serve me literally the left-over burned crumbs of macaroni & cheese from the bottom of a pan that she had taken from underneath the table that roaches came out of. She did not know that I saw that; but, I politely refused it! It was a big to-do because I would not take it; she felt as if I was too good. I felt under no circumstances should she serve me that. Here we are with two different mindsets. *Her* *mindset:* *She thinks that I am too good to eat the scraps from the bottom of the pan. She thinks that I am better than everybody. She thinks that I need to come down off of my high-horse, and that's why nobody likes me.* **My mindset:** *I have always given you the best. I have always treated you like a Queen. I have given your child anything that she has ever requested from me since the day that she was born. I have trained and mentored your child with the secrets of my wisdom that she will carry on for the rest of her life. I have given you fish to eat. I have taught you how to fish. The meal that you are feeding me the crumbs from, is it not I, that taught you how to get it? Is it not from my wisdom that you glean, is it not from my ideas that you have used to purchase what you have fed everyone else, but the one person that would give you the shirt off their back? Is it not because of me that you now provide for your household, and I ask for nothing in return but for you to succeed in life? Have I not been your shoulder to cry on? Have I ever mistreated you one day in your entire life? Have I ever said one discouraging word to you? Have I ever given you any reason to make you feel that I would not be there for you? Have I not shown you unconditional love? Would I not go hungry so you could eat? Is it not I that you should have fed first, is it not I that you should have blessed your seed with? Is it not I that you should have blessed your future with? Is it not I that you should have shown compassion to due to my frail condition? The only reason that you have found to feed me the contaminated crumbs from the bottom of a pan is that you are not happy with the fact that I have been marked for greatness; and I hold myself to a higher standard mentally, physically, emotionally, and spiritually. I know you secretly desire to be where I am, and you don't understand why God has chosen me among all the women in the world for this task, and you are doing this to show me how it feels to be considered less than. Well, it is not my fault if you chose not to succeed* *in the area that you are gifted in, because I have given you every opportunity to succeed in life. You are sitting under great wisdom, but you refused it. The ones that I gave less wisdom, less mentoring, and less everything, did more with what I gave them; and, every single one of them are professionals in their field; and they are absolutely grateful. You have instant access to a fountain to build any dream that you could ever dream, but you refused it—your pride will not allow you to embrace it. People would give anything to be where you are, but there is no value—you have the nerve to humiliate me in my weakest moment. I tell you, when I am weak, then I am strong, only ENVY and JEALOUSY could cause a person to treat someone as such. I forgive you, not just for your sake, but for mine as well; and, this is the very reason why God has chosen me for this mission—I am quick to forgive. What everyone considered as the greatest weakness, God considered the greatest strength; therefore, granting me an anointing of Supernatural Wisdom that penetrates the heart of those who dare to believe.*

I had never been so insulted in my entire life regarding a situation as such. Although I am very picky about my food; however, that was the lowest. At first, I could not get that situation out of my head; because through her eyes, she saw nothing wrong. She saw that I was the problem. I accepted total responsibility for my role in the situation; however, I just choose not to eat that way, and I choose not to live like that. To each his own, but that is just a choice for me, and I am entitled to that. I prayed asking God how I could create a win-win situation out of something like that. He kept saying that I had it. I was confused a little, but when I took my emotions out of that situation, then I was able to see clearly. God was telling me, that I had to follow the Trail of Breadcrumbs that were being laid for me. I had to gather the Breadcrumbs that were being left behind as a lesson or a tool, discard the Breadcrumbs that I did not need, and move on to regain my POWER. For me, I firmly believe in creating a win-win situation out of everything; and, it is that situation that gave birth to "The Breadcrumb Series."

It took someone that I love dearly, to try to serve me the crumbs of Roach Infested Macaroni & Cheese, in a time of my life when I was not feeling at my best, to draw the power of "The Breadcrumb Series" out of me. This is indeed a Win-Win situation that will save and inspire the lives of millions to the end of time. It cannot get any better than that! Now, that's an affliction to laugh about, what was once my favorite dish, can no longer touch my lips—that's how easily we can become scarred by a Breadcrumb. So operate in integrity doing everything in the Spirit of Excellence, and watch how the doors of blessings swing wide-open for you.

57th Type of Person to Avoid

Avoid People Who Are Unaccountable To Change

Things change around us and within us as the seasons do. The problem with us is that we try to stop the season or make the season come before it's time, defying divine order. God did not intend for anything to stay the same, and that includes you! Stop trying to change everyone else and allow God to change you. Whenever you get into the mentality that everyone else needs to change, that is an automatic sign that you have issues within yourself that need to be worked on. As a matter of fact, people become a little insecure and rebellious when or if you try to change everything about them. Furthermore, you are only fooling yourself if you think you can change someone else without you changing YOU! When you change, then others will change; until then, you are fighting a losing battle.

Accountability is the first seed of substance that allows the tree of success to grow inside of you. Growing is one aspect of life but growing properly is another. Most often, we focus on outer growth and forget about the growth that takes place on the inside of us. Unfortunately, if the inner growth is forgotten about, it becomes devastating to the management and accountability of everyday life. In so many words, your life will begin to spiral out of control when change is required of you; it is indeed the Cycle of Life.

It is easier to shift your accountability over to other people, but all this does is cause you to become codependent. Codependency stunts the growth of all who fall into its trap. Yes, it is nice to have people to help you and to do nice things for you. However, when you depend on others to make you happy, eventually it will create problems in your life. In fact, once you become accountable for your own life, the generosity of your own solutions will become inevitable.

When dealing with others regarding becoming accountable for the changes in their lives, our goal is to understand where they are; but, if they refuse to help themselves, leave them alone—don't force them to change or violate their will. Those who have a desire to change for the better, they will; and, those who do not want to change, they will not regardless of what we do.

58th Type of Person to Avoid

Avoid People Who Are Not Generous

If you run into a miser, RUN. Nothing teaches character better than generosity. Nevertheless, with generosity, comes with its twin sibling called reciprocity—they are inseparable twins that serve their own unique purpose. In fact, generosity is the first-born of what you give out positively or negatively and reciprocity is the second-born the holds the leg of its firstborn sibling until its birth order is complete. In so many words, what we give out generously, reciprocity will bring back in full circle in due season, regardless of whether it's positive or negative. We very rarely hear about reciprocity, but it is by far the "Golden Rule" principle of giving and receiving. Of course, it is more than just giving money—it's giving your time, knowledge, wisdom, and most of all, the more familiar adage of, "Do unto others as you would have them to do unto you." Using people to get what you want is the quickest way to lose it. Conniving and scheming to get people to do stuff for you is not the way to get things done. People will naturally help you if you just ask for it. It is okay to ask for help, but the quickest way to receive help is to give it freely.

Giving has much more power and authority than you

will ever possess. The more you give, the more life will be able to give back to you. In so many words, what you give out is an investment in your future that will return to you multiplied many times over. For that reason, you must make sure that you always give out goodness and not evil. It is always best to find a way to invest into someone's life, and someone will eventually invest in you.

59th Type of Person to Avoid

59ᵗʰ Type of Person to Avoid

Avoid People Who Will Divorce You Over Anything

Over the course of truly living a blissful life, we will find that no one has immunity from temptation. It does not matter who we think we are, how much money we have, or how much God we have inside of us. We have been conditioned to think that divorce is the solution to cheating, which is so far from the truth. Divorce has a way of creating a wound that time will only heal. We don't like to talk about divorce; it's just something that we are conditioned to do when one or both parties choose not to work something out. Actually, it has become the easy way out when we feel trapped, unsatisfied or unhappy.

When we lose faith in our relationship or marriage, infidelity has a way of calling our name. Most often, we will not admit that we have lost faith in our relationship; however, it's established in our actions. As we are often taught to look down on cheaters, but why are so many people getting hurt by something that we are taught to reframe from? Or, better yet, why are there so many Christians getting a divorce? This happens when we set our own standards in a relationship; in so many words, we determine the needs of our spouse without asking them. Christians are hiding behind the bible and not taking care of their husbandly or wifely duties. They also use God as a tool to crucify or disrespect their mate for doing something physically that they may have been doing emotionally, mentally, or spiritually.

I feel very strongly that whether you are a Christian or not, relationship restoration is imperative before moving on to another relationship. Regardless of whether you are the cheater or cheatee, you need to discuss and understand the reason behind the actions of the cheater. People cheat for a reason, and cheating is one way that helps them deal with their inner frustrations or lack. However, it's your responsibility to find out what's lacking; if not, history may repeat itself. The most common reason why people cheat is because of sex; however, it could also be the lack of appreciation, the lack of listening, the lack of emotional support, the lack of communication, the lack of security, the lack of money, the lack of power, the lack of sex appeal, or constantly being judged. Whatever it is, you must find it, understand it, and work on it if you can't resolve it. If you need counseling, get it.

Of course, you should not throw away a great relationship because of one mistake. If your partner, spouse, or mate came clean and   assumed responsibility for his or her infidelity and you want to restore the relationship, then why not? In order to properly move on, you must however, repair the broken bonds of trust, vowing to forgive and forget. Of course, it may take a little time to forgive or forget; however, you must never bring up this act of infidelity again. Even though, it may become tempting, do not live in the past when you have made a choice to move on with your relationship. If you cannot forgive or forget, then you should let go of the relationship!

There may come a time in your life when you may become faced with a compromising situation, but always remember that there is hope, healing, and restoration in all things. The story about David & Bathsheba always comes to mind when I think about how we compromise ourselves without knowing it.

David, the King of Israel, had a little too much time on his hands one evening. As a result, he decides to walk out on his balcony where he saw this gorgeous woman bathing. Instead of him finding something else to do, he sat there and watched. David took an interest in this woman; therefore, he started asking questions. He was told that she was the wife of Uriah. Instead of David casting down the thoughts of Bathsheba, he began fantasizing about being with her.

Bathsheba was definitely David's type of woman, and he wanted to get to know her a little better. So, in Bathsheba's time of loneliness, she was invited to his house. She accepted the invitation out of obligation. Even though David abused his authority to seduce Bathsheba, she did put herself in the situation, and she did consent to have relations with him. However, they did not expect for her to become pregnant. Now, in order for David to cover up their actions, he plotted the death of Bathsheba's husband.

After Uriah was killed in the heat of battle, David assumed that he would be able to cover-up his affair with Bathsheba, so he married her. Soon thereafter, the child that was conceived died as punishment for their sin. David & Bathsheba knew that they had made a mistake, and they accepted responsibility for their actions. After doing so, they were able to accept the loss of their child, as they quickly picked up the pieces of their life. God did provide restoration; He gave them another son who found favor in His sight.

Despite the seductive affair, David & Bathsheba later gave birth to Solomon, who was considered to be the wisest King that ever lived. However, he did follow in his father's footsteps, in stature, wisdom, favor, and lust. As a matter of fact, Solomon was a ruler and king by day but a wild lustful man behind closed doors. Yet, it would have been fine, if he had not abused it! I must say, women were his weakness and the key to his downfall; as a result, he lost his Kingdom because He never overcame the desire or lust for foreign women. How wise is that? The wisest man on record, but yet still a man! His father is after God's own heart, but still a mere man! So, how strong are we, when life calls our name?

Have you ever had an overwhelming desire for something that was strictly forbidden? Did the desire consume your every thought? As we have already established in the previous chapters, there is temptation in every woman, and there is temptation in every man; however, the difference is that we must not allow ourselves to become enticed with the entertainment of the forbidden fruit. Yes, you may appear strong, but if you are constantly entertaining the thought of the temptation, it may cause you to fall short in your time of weakness. David was a man after God's own heart, and he fell short in the area that he entertained. This story has indeed left a legacy of great wisdom for all who desire to learn from it. Their legacy tells us that if we have fallen short or someone else has fallen short:

- Do not become emotional about it.
- Do not become anxious.
- Do not become a victim of circumstance.
- Do not become confrontational.
- Do not gossip about your ordeal with your friends.
- Do not make rash decisions.
- Do not continue to badger the cheater about his or her mistake.
- Do not become a cheater yourself.
- Do not go through his or her stuff.
- Do know what you want and what you will not tolerate.
- Do remember that everything is not about you.
- Do acknowledge God and allow Him to direct your path.
- Do look within self, regarding why your partner cheated
- Do understand why you attracted him or her in your life.

- Do look at the big picture of why the two of you came together.
- Do forgive regardless of whether he or she is right or wrong.
- Do communicate with the cheater.
- Work it out if necessary or leave it alone.
- Do understand that time will heal all wounds.
- Do continue to walk in love.

In spite of what brought you and your spouse, mate, or partner together, becoming too emotional will break you apart, if you choose not to resolve a situation or circumstance in the spirit of love. A relationship needs trust, love, commitment, forgiveness, honesty, and balance. When an affair is committed, there is an underlying issue that needs to be resolved. Opening up to your partner to tell them what's wrong may very well be a hard thing to do. Nevertheless, if you don't learn how to respond to the needs of your mate, you may lose something or someone you love and cherish deeply. FYI, it is hard to continue to love someone who does not love you enough to stop cheating on you; and when that spouse leaves, then the shoulda, coulda, and woulda will not work anymore." Sometimes we don't realize how much of a good thing we have until it is gone.

60th Type of Person to Avoid

Avoid People Who Will Not Admit Mistakes

It is best to avoid people who make excuses or blame others for their shortcomings. In any type of relationship, it is best to learn how to own our faults; if we make a mistake, own it; if we fall short, own it. Understand that we will make mistakes—that's inevitable! Most often, at some point in our lives, we find it hard to admit that we may have made a mistake. The keyword here is to ADMIT. Refusing to admit mistakes will contradict or compromise a person's ability to learn, adapt, and adjust to change.

Make no mistake about it, just because a bad decision is made in climbing up the wrong tree, does not necessarily mean that a wrong decision was made. It is possible to make the right decision to do the wrong thing! In doing so, it will do 2 things: 1. BREAK YOU. 2. MAKE YOU. In so many words, God will break you out of your old habits or limitations, and put you back together by transforming you into a person of substance. Easier said than done, right? But it is doable! For the simple fact that you never, ever want to bear fruit in the wrong tree; because, bearing fruit in the wrong tree, could be devastating if you allow the bad or wrong fruit to take root in your heart. Better yet, start listening and allowing your conscience to become your guide as you wait on God to synchronize your heart and your mind.

61st Type of Person to Avoid

Avoid People Who Make a Fool Out of You

Why do we need to forgive someone who is constantly making a fool out of us? Forgiveness is a must, in order for us to move on mentally, emotionally, and spiritually. We do not forgive someone for their sake; we forgive them for our own sake! So, what if we feel like a fool for forgiving? In my opinion, what makes us more of a fool is when we give someone power over our lives by controlling us when we have the power to disengage.

Why would we want to torture ourselves when it's obvious that the person that we are holding a grudge against is living happily ever after or doing their own thing; and, we are torturing ourselves in our own emotions or allowing them to get in our head? Come on; it is not wise to cause ourselves to suffer when we have the option to live in freedom if we simply forgive and let go. When we hit the RESET button on our emotions making a choice to forgive, we are better able to glean from the vestibule of grace and mercy when it's our turn to be forgiven. It is not a matter of IF we need forgiveness; it's a matter of WHEN.

We are all a work in progress, regardless of how well we paint the picture; therefore, we must exercise our God-given right to forgive to ensure that when we fall short, grace and mercy becomes a shield to cover us even when we cannot foresee the wiles of the enemy. I am not saying that we will not get angry, but "Be angry, yet do not sin. Do not let the sun set while you are still angry," according to Ephesians 4:26. If we need to vent, go ahead and do so. By the time the sun sets in the west, so should our anger, and forgiveness should reside in our heart, before we go to bed to ensure that we are able to have peace while we are sleeping. Unforgiveness is the main contributor to what we call insomnia; therefore, we must cleanse our soul of this negative emotion as soon as possible.

Do I have my moments? Absolutely! There are times when I just want to stay mad, especially when my kindness is taken as a weakness. I have trained myself so well until I cannot stay mad for long, even if I try—I will forget about being mad, because my mind will automatically move on to a happy state superseding my emotions. Therefore, once the Spirit of Forgiveness becomes a part of who we are, grudges are less likely to be held against someone; unless, there has been a severe psychological trauma that has occurred that would cause that individual to temporarily harbor unforgiveness. However, in order to move beyond any type of trauma, forgiveness must take place whether it's a part of our character or not. It is okay to hit that reset button on your emotions, on your forgiveness, or your favor, it is a gift that can be utilized at any given moment. Forgive those who have trespassed against you to ensure that you are able to be forgiven.

CHAPTER 11

The Vujá Dé Roar

What does it take to win? In order to win, we must have the desire to do so; and, we must also have our gratefulness intact as well. If we are not grateful for our successes in life, they will appear as failures due to our mindset. It is imperative that we have a winning attitude in the midst of what appears to be a loss as well, because there are times when we will not win physically. But, we must win mentally and emotionally to ensure that we are able to create a win-win situation in order to make the appropriate corrections necessary.

In my opinion, becoming a loser or winner is basically a mindset—we will win to lose and lose to win to complete the cycle of learning. This is where **VUJÁ DÉ** comes into play—**VUJÁ DÉ** is basically the opposite of déjà vu. This is where you are able to see your life from a different PERSPECTIVE. When you are able to shift the perspective on your life, you are then able to shift your vision; therefore, creating a more desirable result rather than having history to repeat itself constantly, wasting precious time. If you do not shift your perspective, your life will continue the same cycle, with different scenes, characters, etc. ending with the same results. Make no mistake about it, if the same thing keeps happening, there is a lesson that you are not learning. Let me say this, you are indeed REQUIRED to shift your perspective to get a different result. Trust me; it's not them, it's not "IT"—it is YOU!

It is through the process of learning and understanding that we become WISE. I will also say this, "It is okay to lose something or someone that's not good for us, or that will drain the life out of us." We cannot win all the time, and we will not lose all the time; however, if we believe that we are a winner at heart, and we perfect the skills of a winner, we will definitely win at more things than we will lose. We attract what we think about all the time, but winning is also a developmental process as well. We cannot sit around talking the game of a winner and not produce the results of a winner. We must work on ourselves every day, set goals, and work toward an end result of winning instead of living our lives like playing lotto or the luck of the draw, expecting great things to happen—real winning does not work like that!

Throughout my journey, I have found that winning is comprised of diligence, humility, compassion, and integrity; and, without it, one must question his or her MOTIVE for the appearance of superficial winning! Manipulating, conniving, scheming, and using people to get what we want are qualities that are NOT conducive to building lasting POWER of a truly winning personality. This type of individual quickly breaks the bonds of trust when they are on the losing end; therefore, we must exercise extreme caution when dealing with a person possessing this type of personality.

We need an awareness of why we are winning, we need an understanding of what it's going to take to win, we must be willing to do everything in the Spirit of Excellence, we need the motivation to win, especially when we want to give up, and we must be willing to pray while trusting the gift from within to supply all our needs. Real winners will not brag about being a winner; they simply get down to business and make things happen creating a win-win situation out of everything, without settling for defeat from the naysayers who are stuck on negative, stuck on material gain, or stuck on pimping them out to break their focus. It takes YOU to win—it is just a thought away, so create a win-win situation out of a negative one and don't be afraid to let go of what or who is not drawing out the winner inside of you.

62nd Type of Person to Avoid

Avoid People Who Set You Back

Overcoming a setback has to become a mindset; if not, one will continue to live that setback over and over again without doing anything about it. In my opinion, setbacks are hidden lessons to bring us into the classroom of life. If we do not understand what God is trying to say to us, what God is trying to teach us, what direction God is trying to lead us in, what corrections that we need to make in our lives, or what has become god in our lives over Him, that lesson will continue to repeat itself until we get it. Therefore, there is no reason to blame anyone for our setbacks—it's never about them, it's always about us.

We have to look from within to find the lesson, and once we find the lesson, it is wrapped in Divine Wisdom. Listen to me, a setback for me is wisdom being handed to me on a silver platter—I eat it up, and I share it to activate the Law of Reciprocity. I was told that I need to break what I'm saying down so that a little child can understand—so, let me explain. When I am served a setback, obstacle, or difficult situation, I become a student, learning the lesson from it; and then, I turn around to become the teacher to empower others to open the floodgate of wisdom. Seed, time, and harvest apply to our setbacks as well; and it cannot hold us back if we simply set it up to become a blessing for ourselves and others. If we can find a way to learn from our setbacks and create a win-win situation by looking for the positive without focusing on the negative, wisdom will be waiting to provide us with the substance or provisions needed to overcome the situation, circumstance, or event.

In my opinion, a setback is a distraction to keep us blind, confused, and frustrated with ourselves; nevertheless, when we exercise wisdom, compassion, and due diligence when dealing with a setback, we are better able to maneuver around obstacles to achieve our desired goals. Here is a prime example, if we crush an ant mound, we will never see them weeping or settling for defeat—they will rebuild that mound by any means necessary regardless of whether we want them there or not; it is sad to say, but it is only death that will stop an ant from rebuilding its empire. If something or someone rains on our parade, simply dry off, regroup, get a strategy, and go for it again!

A true winner will not stop because of a setback; they simply find another way. Leave no stone unturned; regardless of how it may appear. Your best bet is to refrain from settling for defeat mentally, do what you have to do to overcome your setbacks emotionally, and keep yourself moving physically, to ensure that you do not have any regrets about giving up on YOU. Oh by the way, if you add a little prayer to it, you will indeed enhance your Spiritual Powerhouse causing the spirit of defeat to flee. Yes, prayer is like the icing on the cake that bridges the triumphant gap commencing all things to work together for your good.

CHAPTER 12

Roaring Kryptonite

As adults, we do not often reveal our need to be touched, but let me tell you this—there is a little child in every woman or man that needs to be nurtured. If one does not get it—there is a longing from within, and the one that comes along to nurture that little child from within, getting them to smile while finding that happy place, will become that person's KRYPTONITE! This can work positively or negatively; but, make no mistake about it, everyone has their kryptonite, if left unchecked. If you have not met your kryptonite yet, keep living!

Setting boundaries with the right response will keep you in control, regardless of what occurs in your life. This is where balance and integrity come into the picture—having self-control will remove the limits on what you can achieve, as long as you do not get entangled in a web of kryptonic behavior.

63rd Type of Person to Avoid

Avoid People Who Procrastinate

The past is not designed to be used as a crutch; it is to be used as a stepping stone. Crutches are basically excuses that leave room for procrastination or taking the easy way out. For the most part, it is very, very hard to achieve anything when we are complacent with doing nothing; besides, it takes up too much energy thinking, worrying or pondering about an excuse anyway.

We all have a natural instinct inside of us that seeks to be understood; especially, by the ones we love. Not to mention, we all have different perceptions, purposes, opinions, and priorities that need to be respected. Of course, understanding can be a lot of things, but it is not rationalizing or judging. As a matter of fact, it is having the patience to see beyond our own point of view.

Victories are won by overcoming our fears, limitations or setbacks with our undivided attention. When our attention is divided, it is very hard to take risks or overcome setbacks. When we are satisfied with the way things are, we tend to avoid taking risks—when taking a risk is necessary to get us to the next level. The best way to start gaining control over our lives is to start controlling what enters our eye gates, ear gates, and what enters or exits the gate of our mouth. As a matter of fact, we often take for granted these

3 gates of entry until our lives spiral out of control. Trust me, an out of control life is not a life of victorious living and not being able to satisfy the one you claim to love is not victorious living as well.

64th Type of Person to Avoid

Avoid People Who Do Not Prepare

Winging it in life is not going to get it! Winging it in a relationship is not going to get it! A victorious life takes preparation, determination, and sacrifice, which are extremely important when it comes down to making the right move at the right time and taking care of the needs of our mate. In addition, our determination begins with us imagining ourselves succeeding or becoming victorious at whatever we do, especially in the bedroom. Of course, determination is all mental; particularly when we cannot see, feel, or touch our determination; however, we **CAN** see, feel and touch the results of our determination. So, make sure that you keep your mind focused and free of unwanted distractions, to ensure that God places your divine connections where they need to be at the right time to prevent the loss of your spouse out of carelessness or irresponsibility.

65th Type of Person to Avoid

Avoid The Sugar Daddies and Sugar Mamas

When we do not please our spouse sexually, we increase the risk of being cheated on. We are created with wants, desires, and needs, if we refuse to take care of the needs of our spouse or mate, they may not cheat physically, but definitely emotionally or mentally. When a relationship is missing something, there is a possibility that a spouse will seek refuge, romance or intimacy from someone else out of hostility, immaturity, revenge, or addiction. Is it fair to blame a cheater for cheating if we don't handle our responsibility as a woman or man to keep him or her satisfied? Of course, this is a catch-22 question, but we must answer it at some point in our relationship; especially, if the relationship is over 5 years old. If you are not ready to answer that question right now, let's see what Jake has to say about it:

Jake was a well-respected Senator, who believed in fighting for what's right. He also helped a lot of non-profit organizations in the minority community; however, being an older man, he was also known for flirting with the young, pretty girls. Jake would often mention that pretty girls were eye-candy to the sore eyes. It took me years to understand what Jake was referring to, until I met his wife. Jake's wife, Tilly, felt as if Jake owed her something. Tilly was very abrasive with Jake in front of guests, friends, and family members. She was very anti-social, and she treated the Senator, our great

Senator, like a piece of dirt. I could only imagine what she was like in the bedroom! However, I did notice that Tilly was only nice to her children, which shocked me. So, I made it my business to befriend Tilly and probe her for information on why she treated Jake the way she did.

Over a period of time, I got to really know Tilly. I found that Tilly was actually a very nice woman; however, she hated the fact that her husband was a public figure. She felt as if his job took him away from her, so she cut him off sexually. Once she cut Jake off sexually; he cut her off emotionally. He began to look at the young, lean and sexy women; as a matter of fact, Jake openly took pleasure in looking at other women without sparing her feelings at all. As a result, Jake indulged himself in his new found fetish, and he no longer desired her. Jake paid the bills, recognized her as the mother of his children, and that's it! Tilly felt stuck, she did not want to break up her home, and she did not want to give up her lifestyle, so she resorted to anger, bitterness, hostility, hatred, resentment, and fear. She stated that she would prefer to live in anger bearing the psychological consequences of a cheating spouse than to live a life of poverty.

Tilly regrets the day that she cut her husband off sexually because now her husband takes pleasure in having other women to do what she wasn't willing to do. And, now that she is willing to do it, he doesn't want it. Tilly's husband, became addicted to cheating because she tried to punish him by withholding sex and now it has backfired on her. What she thought would cause him pain, has become his gain.

Tilly tried to cheat, but she fears losing everything. So, she lives in luxury and deals with her cheating spouse the best way she knows how.

Jake is now retired, spending even more time away

from home. Tilly is still dealing with Jake's infidelity; however, she finally gained enough balls to find a friend with benefits. The funny thing about it all, Tilly became a Cougar, because her friend that she was receiving benefits from, was half her age.

The restriction game can indeed backfire, so be very cautious when using your sexuality as a weapon. Nevertheless, no one deserves to be cheated on, no matter what's going on in the relationship. As we all know, cheating hurts regardless of how tough we may have become. When the excitement of a relationship dies down, we must find new and exciting ways to keep the fire burning within ourselves, as well as in the relationship. However, if one person is doing all the work, eventually he or she will get tired—it's just a matter of time before that kryptonite avails itself, if left unchecked.

In order to better a relationship, we must express our lack of excitement, giving the other person the opportunity to work on it or to express their feelings, or the lack thereof. It's imperative that we give our spouse, mate, or partner an opportunity to work on an area that could pose a potential danger.

66th Type of Person to Avoid

Avoid People Who Want The Benefits Without A Commitment

Chapter 12 | Ruby Fleurcius

On the other side of the potential dangers of the Sugar Daddies and the Sugar Mamas, we have the benefits! We often keep the act of cheating to a minimum by creating friendships. Having friends allow us to have several friends at the same time without someone feeling the sting of being cheated on. However, if you are having sex with your friends, then is he or she really a friend? Friends usually appreciate each other socially and emotionally with no strings attached. Now, when we start adding the benefits into the equation, the appreciation becomes physical, emotional, and sometimes social. Having a friend with benefits is nothing more than having an open relationship, or a "Booty Call" for the horny, lonely, and the desperate. Of course, having an open relationship or answering a "Booty Call" is commonly frowned upon, but it is quite common now-a-days. Furthermore, this is a great way to try it before you buy it, because if he or she does not satisfy you, then there is no need to waste your time.

If you don't know what you want, then you should have an open relationship. However, if you have what you want, having a friend with benefits is a great way to legally cheat on your mate. This is why we are becoming so caught up with multiple relationships that are providing little or no substance besides sex or a superficial prostitution ring for those who choose to sell themselves short. Check out this story:

Pat and Frank met at the library on her Birthday. She was so excited about meeting him; she assumed he was her birthday present from God. Frank appeared to be the man of her dreams, he cooked, cleaned, pampered, and catered to her; she had finally found a man that she could relate to. He really knew how to rope her in, and she fell for it.

One morning Pat had to make a quick trip to the other side of town, so she calls Frank from her cell phone and somehow the lines cross. She was able to hear Frank candidly talking to another woman as if he was dating her as well. Pat could not believe how candidly she heard his whole conversation. A few minutes later, Pat called Frank again, he answered. She explained how she heard his conversation with another woman; and, of course, he didn't believe her. She then asked if she could stop by; he claimed that he did not have time to entertain her company, not realizing that she had just heard him invite someone else over. Therefore, she knew that he was up to no good. After several months of keeping Frank at arm's length, she allowed him to stop by to bring her dinner. Afterward, he walked outside to make a phone call, and she could hear him screaming at what appeared to be another woman, but she did not want to jump to any conclusions. He walked back in her house as if nothing ever happened, had sex with her and then left. Pat felt so dirty; she did not expect him to leave right away, she thought that he would at least hold her all night. And, not only that, she did not hear from him for a whole week; Pat was on this emotional rollercoaster with her emotions because Frank was treating her like a prostitute; He would feed her, expect sex from her and then leave, not calling her until he wanted another sexual fix.

Like clockwork, Frank called a week later wanting to take Pat out to lunch; she reluctantly declined, because she felt as if Frank only wanted one thing. She then asked him about their relationship and he responded, "We are just friends and whatever happens, happen." After he had made that statement, she knew that he had

Chapter 12 | Ruby Fleurcius

played her for a fool. She was having sex for love, and he was having sex for fun, so much for a friend with benefits! As a result, his actions taught her how to think and act like a man, while maintaining her glamour and glitz without giving up her goodies while being the 2nd woman prostitute. She is now on the "No Commitment, No Goodies" plan.

Pat believes that if women are able to keep their legs closed long enough, they are better able to tell if a man is interested in them or if they just want sex. She firmly believes that there is no need to stay in an unfaithful, unfulfilling, and uncommitted sexual relationship with someone who could care less if she had a pot to piss in. Pat later found out that Frank firmly believes in the "Friends with Benefits Theory" and that's why he is still single.

The key to the "Friends with Benefits Theory"
In order to make the friends with benefits theory work, both parties must be in 100% total agreement with it. If one person wants a relationship and one person wants a friendship with a little nookie on the side, it's not going to work. Someone is going to get their feelings hurt, or someone is going to feel used or manipulated.

This is a very promiscuous type of relationship, and extreme caution needs to be exercised when having casual sex with multiple partners. However, it will work for you if you just want to have sex without the baggage of relationship complications, the responsibility of a commitment, or when you are dealing with a person "who does not have it like that." Just remember that anyone that you are having sex withholds the possibility of you developing an emotional bond, especially if the sex is good. For that reason, you must set up rules, boundaries, and limitations to ensure that you both are on one accord.

If you are on the FWB (Friend With Benefits) program, make sure that you are not using the words: honey, baby, sweetheart, dear, sweet thing, boo, my boo, sweetie pie, I love you, etc. to ensure that your "Bed-Buddy" does not become your "Bugaboo." It may cause things to become a little complicated if one person starts to develop more feelings than the other. Also, be very cautious when introducing your FWB to your friends and family members, it really complicates things. Plus, this should be your secret anyway, because FWB is no more than a free sex service and you never want to ruin your credibility around the people that you love and respect.

Those who settle for the FWB blah, blah, blah. You may get hurt. When a person does not value your feelings, then more than likely he or she will not value your body, meaning your sex is going to play-out real quick. If someone can run in and out of your body with no emotions, just think about what he or she could do to your heart once the thrill is gone. FYI, your body is your temple; so, you make a decision on how much value you place on it. Besides, more than likely, when your FWB finds that special someone that does not settle for the FWB arrangement; trust me, you might as well kiss him or her good-bye.

Just Friends and No Benefits

Chapter 12 | *Ruby Fleurcius*

This is the way to go if you really want to have a successful friendship between a male and a female. A relationship that started out as totally plutonic friends will have a better chance at succeeding than any other relationship across the board. This type of relationship allows you to get to know a person mentally and emotionally first. Therefore, the relationship is not based on lust. If your relationship cannot survive without any physical contact, foreplay, going out, affection, gifts, etc.; then you may want to question that relationship. This is the very reason why the friends without benefit theory work best for those who really want to attract his or her soul mate. When someone is your best friend, you are able to communicate with them better than just being lovers.

67th Type of Person to Avoid

Avoid People Who Take You For Granted

When we become comfortable in a relationship, we tend to take a lot of things for granted. Actually, we subconsciously get into a comfort zone, thinking that we do not have to work on our relationship. For that reason alone, people are just throwing away great relationships, thinking that a relationship will work on its own. The truth of the matter is, anything that's worth having, we must work on it and work at it, regardless of how many years we've invested. As a matter of fact, vested years should give us more of a reason to keep things fresh, new, and exciting.

Comfort zones can be formed in many different areas. Most often, when we are in a relationship, we tend to neglect our appearance or the things that attracted that person to us in the first place. Since God created us a certain way, we are indeed stimulated by visual appeal. Our visual appeal is what provokes our natural sense of attraction; therefore, we cannot neglect our personal appearance.

68th Type of Person to Avoid

Avoid People Who Are Lazy

Excuses, excuses, excuses—we all have them. Excuses to be lazy should never be one of them. When we don't want to do something, we make an excuse. When we don't want to go somewhere, we make an excuse. When we don't want to think about something, we make an excuse. When we are late, we make an excuse. When we get caught in a lie, we make an excuse. When we get caught in our folly, we make an excuse. When we do not want to work, we make an excuse. If you haven't made an excuse, just live a little longer, and you will eventually make one. Some people live their lives making excuses for not doing; some people make excuses for not living, and some people make excuses to live. Regardless of the excuse, it does not negate the fact that we must accept responsibility for our actions, reactions, commitments, and the lack thereof. When we become lazy mentally, we often cover it up by uneventful excuses that drive us away from our goal or commitments.

We spend more time trying to figure out how to avoid people, places, and things in our life opposed to preparing ourselves for the great unknown. As a matter of fact, we often limit ourselves by the way we make excuses for not reaching beyond our comfort zone.

Life has a way of blindsiding us with the things that we neglect dealing with; while hitting us below the belt with things that we refuse to deal with. The neglect or the refusal to prepare or cheat-proof our relationship has a way of leaving an open door for excuses. If you want more, you are definitely going to have to prepare for more of what you do have and what you don't have as well. Preparation is the key to excel beyond the limits of your own making.

You must find a way to center your action on the goal and not the excuse. If you are in it to win it, you will find that you will start making progress in the right direction until you cross the finish line of ultimate success in your relationship. From me to you, if you are going to make an excuse, make an excuse to succeed in safeguarding your relationship!

Living our lives in fast forward can and will cause us to jump from one thing to the next and from one person to the next. Besides, jumping into things without preparing ourselves or thinking about what we are doing will cause the best of us to make simple mistakes that could or should have been avoided. Of course, we will not be able to prepare for everything; but, we can prepare or prevent some things from happening!

There are many misconceptions in life and discipline is not one of them. When we allow ourselves to meander through life doing whatever we want without any accountability, we are setting ourselves up for the ultimate disappointment. A carefree and a careless demeanor do not necessarily mean that we don't care; my friend, it's our actions that tell us how much we truly care.

When we find ourselves running from responsibility, rest assured that we would have unresolved issues in that particular area as well. Irresponsibility and recklessness are totally unacceptable. When we become truly responsible for ourselves, we are better able to take responsibility for our relationship; especially, for those whom we proclaim to care about. Of course, with responsibility, there comes discipline.

Discipline is required to achieve anything worth having and without it; we will not get much accomplished. When we find ourselves surrounded by incomplete projects, incomplete relationships, or incomplete anything, our guard should automatically go up. This is a sign of having too many distractions and too many distractions impede our discipline. Furthermore, the lack of discipline leaves room for bad habits to take over and control our lives; and, the one thing we must never do is, lose our ability to govern ourselves mentally, physically, emotionally or spiritually. This will ensure that we are able to build, break-down, restore, preserve, or burn a bridge if necessary, depending

Chapter 12 | *Ruby Fleurcius*

on our situation or circumstance at hand. And, even when things do not go your way, you must look at things from a different perspective. Nevertheless, before I end this chapter, I must tell this story, it will definitely empower you to start what you can finish and finish what you start.

God has blessed Sally with a great job, great home, great husband, and great children; she felt as if she could not ask for anything more. Sally's one of the good girls on the block, she's attractive, sexy, pretty, smart, the girl has some mad skills, except for in the bedroom. Her husband Bill, loves her and could not ask for a better woman, but for some reason, he wasn't sexually satisfied. He expressed his concerns with Sally; but during intercourse, she would still just lay there as if she did not know what to do. Bill did all the work, and he was getting tired and really bored. Sally really felt as if she was taking care of Bill's needs by sexing him whenever he wanted. She did not realize there was a difference between sexing, and pleasing him until she caught him watching a blue movie (Porn).

Sally stopped talking to Bill; she did not have sex with him, she did not cook for him, she did not do anything for him whatsoever. She treated her husband like a dog. Bill tried talking to her, but she would not listen. He bought her gifts; she threw them in the trash. Bill was so hurt; he did not know how to fix this. He came home one day; Sally sat his clothes outside and had changed the locks. Bill begged Sally not to do this, as he sat at the door crying like a baby. Before he left, he said a silent prayer, asking God to work it out, then he politely took his belongings and left.

Bill did not mean to hurt his wife; all he wanted her to do is make an effort to add a little spice to their sex life. He tried calling Sally every day; she would not answer the phone or allow him to speak to the kids. After a couple months of rejection, Bill accepted the fact that Sally did not want anything else to do with him, so he stopped calling.

After Bill stops calling, Sally started feeling lonely and frisky. So she decided to go out with her friends. That night, she ran into one of her ex-boyfriends, and they had a blast. Being that she felt comfortable with her ex, she started hanging out with him; one thing led to another, and they had sex. Afterward, he got up and never called her again. She called him for 3 weeks straight; he would not answer or return her calls. Finally, she got the hint.

A week later, Sally went to the grocery store; and low and behold she runs into her ex-boyfriend. They were shocked to see each other; however, out of curiosity Sally asked him, "Why did you stop calling?" He responded, "We had nothing in common." She said, "What do you mean?" He responded, "That was the worst sex that I ever had in my life, I can't believe that you were married." Sally was so embarrassed; she just walked away.

Sally cried all the way home; she could not believe that she was so naive. She thought she had it going on in the bedroom, and now the joke is on her. She treated her husband like a dog when he was trying to work with her. She could not take it anymore, so she got on her knees to pray. She asked God to teach her how to please her husband. She called Bill later that night to apologize for her actions and ask him to come home. Of course, Bill refused. All Bill wanted to do was see his children.

One day after work, Bill went to see his children. They were so excited to see their Dad, and so was Sally. She called Bill into the room to talk, but talking was the last thing on her mind. Bill could not believe that Sally was seducing him, he could not control himself. Sally had learned a few techniques from that blue movie that she kicked her husband out over. She told Bill not to do anything, that she was going to do all the work, and he needed to show her what he liked. Sally was a woman on a mission; she became serious about pleasing Bill. She wanted her husband back, and she wasn't going to stop at anything until he's back home and satisfied.

After Sally had learned how to lay it on Bill, he came back home with a smile on his face. She really learned how to work that thing; she took video sex courses; she learned how to dance for her husband, and she became a master at pleasing him. She could care less how her parents looked down on oral sex; she just made sure that she was able to do it and do it very well. Bill could not believe that Sally had all of that hidden inside of her. Now, Sally has a different move for every day of the week, and Bill dares not to complain. Sally has indeed rocked Bill's world.

Sally and Bill are so happy together. Sally could not believe that she was about to lose a great husband out of her stubbornness. She really believes that it was the grace of God that taught her how to please her husband properly. Sally is now teaching other women on how to please their man.

The dynamics of achieving success in anything or with anyone, requires us to persevere through our challenges to achieve a common goal. Whatever that common goal is, it's between you and the one you love. However, you cannot force anyone to do that in which they are not willing to do, but you can offer them love, wholeness, respect, and peace.

Plan time with your mate, have a date night, and visualize the type of relationship that you desire with your mate. A relationship of peace, happiness, and love are much desired for those who are seeking true companionship. Take all the negative feelings or thoughts about your relationship and turn them into positive ones. When we develop that mentality, we are better able to cater to our spouse, mate, or partner to ensure that his or her taste buds remain sweet. This is where the power of our negotiation skills comes in.

The power of negotiation works when we have our integrity intact. As a matter of fact, our negotiation skills are greatly enhanced when we master our conflict resolution to incorporate a positive, sweet twist. We are able to pretty much create anything that we desire as long as we are able to extract the positive, and use the negative as a learning tool to enhance our strategic thinking process of creating something pleasant.

CHAPTER 13

Sweet Temptation Roar

Temptation is Sweet; which means that Proverbs 9:17 wasn't lying when it said, "Stolen water is sweet, and bread eaten in secret is pleasant." I have found that the best way to catch a Bee is with honey. If we don't believe in the sugar bait—we will, if we are put in the right situation, with the right person, at the right time, or when we are about to lose our mate to another person, we will not understand. Plus, it is easy to say what we will not do, until our fleshly desires get a taste of something really sweet that our taste buds like…..

The fear of losing gets diluted when you are 100% committed to the success of your relationship or marriage. However, just because you are committed does not mean that temptation does not exist or that your spouse will be 100% committed to the success of the relationship as well. In my opinion, when you become 100% honest with yourself about what you feel, you are better able to deflate that in which is tempting you.

69th Type of Person to Avoid

Avoid People Who Will Not Fight The Temptation Of The Flesh

We all a have secrets, we all have desires, we all have fantasies, and we all have temptations that we dare not act upon or tell anyone about. How do I know, because we are human! We are all tempted with something; if you are not, live a little longer. However, our temptations should never outweigh our victories. Of course, every person thinks he or she is right in his or her own eyes; however, if we search the depths of our soul, we are better able to understand our go's, no's, and pro's of what we are doing, saying or becoming. Besides, most of the individuals who indulge in the act of cheating usually start out very innocently. Now with that being said, I have another story for you:

Jim and Lucy have been happily married for 4 years; about 3 months ago, Lucy's ex-boyfriend retires from the military and moves back to town. Ross, the ex-boyfriend, bumps into Lucy at the local diner; she was so excited to see him that she canceled her 10 o'clock meeting. They sat down for coffee, spending 3 hours reminiscing about the past. She told Ross that she was happily married, and he told her that he was engaged.

Over the next couple of months, Lucy and Ross exchanged emails daily, but Lucy deleted her emails to ensure that her husband did not see them. Lucy and Ross met for lunch several times, but Lucy would always tell her husband that she was meeting her girlfriend for lunch. As Lucy began to feel a little guilty, she was not sure if she should tell her husband about Ross. However, she knew that if she got caught, it would damage her relationship with her husband. And, she did not want to damage her relationship with Ross because he put her through college. She had no intentions of having an affair with Ross; but if she doesn't tell Jim about Ross, it would be considered an affair because she's dishonest with him. As a result, Lucy spent a couple of days trying to figure out how to handle this situation.

So, she decides to tell her husband about Jim, how he helped her through school after her mother died and how she was afraid to tell him about Ross. She explained how she wanted him to meet Ross and his fiancé, and he thought it was a great idea. They met, they got along, and they all became best friends.

Lucy realized that if she wanted Jim to remain her husband, she had to be honest, without putting herself in a position to become tempted. Ross is now married, and he's really thankful to Lucy for teaching him a valuable lesson about being honest. They are all the best of friends doing everything as a group.

It's imperative that we protect ourselves when moving ahead in life. When we move ahead, there will always be those who are designed to get us off track. Most often, it is through our environment or conversations that we lower our guard to people, places, and things that appear to have our back. For that reason, we must evaluate our conversations carefully; because it is through the conversations that we entertain, that gets us side-tracked, even if we are trying to do the right thing in our relationship. We must understand that there are choices all around us, and it's our responsibility to choose the company that we want to keep and the environment we want to strive in.

Now, if there is some form of temptation that has the potential to cause you to suffer great loss, do not and I mean do not, put yourself in a position to become tempted or put yourself in a position to become defiled. Sometimes you can't even entertain certain conversations with certain people, because it is so easy to have an affair without having sex.

Secret meeting such as lunches, dinners, movies, vacations, etc. with a person of the opposite sex without the knowledge of your spouse opens the door of temptation. If you have to hide something like this from your spouse, something is definitely wrong, and you need to reevaluate your intentions. Just entertaining such issues and thoughts lay the foundation for an affair to occur in the mind. Yes, you may be strong; but, once again, you are human! We do make mistakes and for that reason, here are some tips to help you protect yourself:

- Trust yourself to do the right thing.
- Know and understand what you are feeling and why?
- Make sure you are doing it for you and no one else.
- Avoid sexually explicit conversations.
- Watch out for the intimate touching or feeling.
- Guard your heart.

- Don't go near a place you know that will entertain your weakness.
- Don't consume your mind with lustful or perverted thoughts. Replace those thoughts with something constructive and positive.
- Focus on your self-control from the inside out, not the outside in.
- Keep yourself active and busy.
- Pray.

The taste of temptation is real sweet, but we must understand that once the taste for this type of cheating sugar develops, it's extremely hard to put down. Regardless of what type of temptation we are faced with, if we are able to think our way into it, we are able to think our way out.

Our victories are governed by our ability to think, react, and become that in which we were not before. In so many words, we must grow mentally, physically, emotionally, and spiritually through our temptations to ensure that we experience the fullness of victorious living.

Victorious living is within your reach, all you have to do is stay focused with a positive attitude while having an idea of what, when, how, where, and why temptations are designed to come your way. And, if you fall, the last thing you ever want to do is wallow in self-pity when it's so easy to gird up your loins and walk or flow in victorious living. From me to you, it's not the way in which you tell your story when you are tempted that creates victory; it is the way in which you LIVE your story through the temptation that creates victory.

CHAPTER 14

The Mind of Mastery R.O.A.R.

Is "Doing You" really worth it? Yes and No! Yes, if we are doing positive, productive things to take ourselves to the next level, then "Doing You" is worth the effort. However, the answer is "No" if we are doing things to set ourselves back, or causing a great disservice to ourselves and others. In all that we do in life, there will be a little give and take, ups and downs, positives and negatives, or setups and setbacks; but, if what we are doing is taking us in a negative direction—then the "Doing You" colloquialism means that we need to do something else.

"Doing You" is at its best when we allow ourselves to activate the Law of Reciprocity. In my opinion, doing what we want to do cannot be a one-way street—it is designed to provide a benefit to the giver and the taker; therefore, creating a win-win situation. In so many words, in order to get what we want, we must give people what they want. Take a moment to evaluate why you are "Doing You"—if it's all about a selfish act; then you may want to consider doing someone else to prevent the Law of Karma from catching up with your egotistical behavior.

How do we overcome our egotistical behavior? Egos come and go—they are all around us and within us as well. Our ego contributes to our prideful arrogant behavior that causes one to think that they are more than they are or better than certain people based on their power, money, sex, or status. If we pay close attention we will find that our ego has a way of causing us to build a hidden resistance to following instructions; it will also cause us to degrade those who appear not to be up to our standards or beneath us.

A tell-tale sign of a super inflated or busted ego is when a person is driven to compete with others, compare themselves with others all the time, or wanting what others have in order to fit into a certain clique. Is it a bad thing? In my opinion, it really depends on who is looking or who we are hurting. The pride of life has been one of the greatest downfalls of man today; therefore, we must reverse the effect to ensure that we are able to build, mentor, and leave a legacy to empower generations to come, without dividing ourselves as well as the people around us.

Our ego is what places us in a box, and it also will cause us to place others in a box; when we should be empowering and releasing ourselves as well as others out of it. The way that I recognize a confident person is by looking for their humility. True confidence is expressed in our ability to be who we are without bragging or boasting about it, but simply being about it. Our mouth can say a lot of things, but if our actions or reactions are not lining up, then there is a disconnect somewhere; and we need to find it!

A confident person will never have to say a word about his or her confidence. It's indeed a natural occurrence that radiates from within that's revealed in our ability to exhibit love, joy, peace, kindness, goodness, faithfulness, gentleness, and self-control without being told to do so or without giving it a second thought. You cannot go wrong being humble; it is humility that opens the door to Divine Favor in places where the door was completely closed. Trust me, humility is indeed your trump card, especially when you are in need of something that you do not have already or when you have a true desire to "Do You." Carrie is my example:

Carrie spent many years getting over the abandonment of a man that she loved more than God himself. Her ex-fiancé Ricky, walked out on her because she could not keep her weight down. He did not care whether she starved herself or not, all he wanted is for his trophy to be a size 6 or below. Her ex was obsessed with her being a size 6, but when she went to a size 10, he would act as if she was a fat slob and he would tell her that she needed to stop eating. He tortured her mentally. She had a hard time dealing with the fact that he was only in love with her body. But she loved him, and she was willing to give him what he wanted. Carrie took all types of diet pills for years without thinking about the long-term effects of ephedra-based diet pills and drinks. She also went to the extreme of secretly having liposuction done. Carrie went over the hill with this diet thing just to prevent Ricky from cheating on her. When she would visit her parent's house, she could not stop eating; she ate up everything; her parents knew something was wrong, but she would never admit she was bulimic.

One night Ricky got in bed with a t-shirt on, which made Carrie suspicious. She then asked, "Why are you sleeping with a shirt on;

you never did that before?" He reluctantly responded, "It's cold in here." So Carrie did not push the issue. The next morning she went into the bathroom while Ricky was getting out of the shower; she was shocked at what she saw. He had deep scratches all over his back; Carrie just broke down and started crying because she knew that he had been with another woman. Ricky did not offer any type of apology or explanation; he just stepped over her while she was sitting on the floor sobbing. Carrie knew that she should have walked away at that point, but she could not bear the fact of losing her man to another woman because she could not stay off of her eating binges.

This cheating episode pushed Carrie over the deep-end. She would not eat for days; she was an anorexic in denial. She secretly battled anorexia and bulimia on her own. She did not want help because she would have to explain why she was torturing herself over a man. Until one day she was forced to do so when she suffered a heart-attack. All of the diet pills, binging, purging and not eating had caught up with her. She almost died with her little secret and the most amazing thing about this little ordeal; Ricky never came to see her. Although he called, he never came to the hospital to check on her; he just made up some lame excuse to take advantage of the time that she was out of the house. While in the hospital, she did not appear to be anorexic, so the doctor's overlooked that fact, nor did she volunteer any information. However, they did ask her about taking any form of diet pills; of course, she denied it, which caused her heart attack at such a young age to become a mystery to the doctors. Nevertheless, Carrie knew the truth.

After Carrie had gotten out of the hospital, she made a promise to herself that she was not going to take any more diet pills and that she was not going to starve herself anymore. And, by her making that promise to herself, she gained weight. Ricky became uncomfortable with that and did not want to be seen with her. Even though

Carrie felt bad about the way he was treating her, she knew that she had to start loving herself and to become healthy, even if it meant gaining weight and losing her man. Carrie believes as long as she loves herself, she had to let the chips fall where they may. After all of the torture and pain that Carrie endured, she still lost Ricky to another woman anyway. After many years of pain, she finally accepted that it was indeed a part of God's plan for her life.

Carrie was and still is a very pretty young lady; she is still trying to overcome the mental torture that she endured. She is now eating healthy and working out while treating herself really good. Though she is no longer a size 10, she has learned to love the skin she's in as she inspires other women to do the same as well. However, Ricky has his size 2 trophy wife, but still begs Carrie to come back to him. When "Doing You" keep those unwanted distractions under your feet as you focus on loving the skin you are in.

70th Type of Person to Avoid

Avoid People Who Compare You With Others

Carrying the baggage from a previous relationship into a new relationship weighs the relationship down. Especially, when one is comparing the old bags with the new ones—it could leave a bad taste in someone's mouth. There are some things that we may have to expose out of honesty; but, there are some things that we are going to have to leave in the closet and vow to never expose them. Everyone has a past, but we never allow our past to prevent us from embracing our future. If one is done with the old, put it away and enjoy the new.

Comparing is one of the biggest time wasters known to man; while at the same time, measuring has proven to be one of the biggest time-maximizers. Actually, they are sort of the same, but very different in their very own unique way; therefore, creating a very thin line between the two. Comparing is indeed a form of measurement, but the difference is the MOTIVE behind it. Typically, comparing is used to examine, justify, or rationalize based on an individual's perception that usually create limits; whereas, measuring is based more on facts that typically heightens the growth of an individual. Furthermore, measuring allows us to set reasonable boundaries to maximize our effectiveness that will produce something positive and productive. When setting goals, measuring is a prerequisite! With that being said, comparing ourselves with others is not an option; we must find a way to avoid this at all cost.

Player hating or playing one person against another is definitely someone that needs to be avoided at all cost—this is a perfect sign of a trouble-maker.

71st Type of Person to Avoid

Avoid People Who Rush All The Time

How do we get things accomplished when there is not enough time in the day? Time management is the one thing that most of us take for granted. In my opinion, time is on our side, and if we give it the opportunity to serve us, it will provide us with enough time to get things done with time left over. When we rush, rush, rush, we cannot say that we accomplish more, but we can say that we make more mistakes when we do rush. If this is happening, this is where setting priorities come into play—I have found that creating a To-Do list really helps to keep us on track or to get back on track when necessary.

We must be able to deal with change when our To-dos are disrupted, and we must be able to get back on track without allowing our emotions or our mind to become the Devil's playground. In so many words, we cannot overthink issues when our To-dos become little boo-boos! Safeguarding our mind is a prerequisite to gaining control over our time—we all have the same amount of time in the day, it's how we manage it that creates the lack or abundance.

How can we change our mindset toward time? I am so glad to answer that question! I have found that the best way to manage our time is to relax in it. If we find peace in the midst of our busyness, it will grant us the ability to think clearly, set priorities, and provide a way to manage our reactions or actions when we have a disruption. Most often, when we make others feel as if we are too busy for them, they subconsciously pull away; eventually causing a disconnect in the relationship. Even if we are busy, we must find a way to take a moment to give those we love our undivided attention;

it only takes a fraction of a second to show an individual that they are more important than what really has our attention.

The mismanagement of time has caused more broken relationships than we would care to imagine—the truth is........if social media is getting more time than our family or if social media is getting more time than the ones that truly have our back, then we must reevaluate the management of our time. Trust me, if there is something that we want to really do or someone that we really want to see, we will make time by any means necessary.

Excuses about not having enough time are just that, AN EXCUSE! If something or someone is not a part of our To-Do's, own it, and be so kindly to put it on the To-Don't list. You do not have to make an excuse for wasting time on people, places, and things that are not conducive to where you are going or what you want to do.

CHAPTER 15

The Happiness Roar

Struggles are a part of life—without a struggle to get or keep something or someone, value cannot legitimately become established. Plus, we cannot really determine who is really with us, until a struggle or a set-back is presented in our life. The most valuable elements of life are derived from some sort of struggle; better yet, the most dynamic testimony originated from a struggle, the most successful company started with a struggle, etc. Trust me, it is the struggles in life that makes us who we are, as well as help us to understand why we are.

Although we cannot change the struggles that we may have had during our lifetime; however, we can change our perception of our experience, and we can also find our happy place as well. As people, places, and things flow in and out of your life, allow the struggle to enable you to become a better person, and not a bitter one. All you have to do is embrace your ability to become a happy person—it's just that simple.

It does not matter what life throws at you, all you have to do is go back to that happy place mentally and emotionally; and then eventually, the physical will meet up with what you see in your mind's eye. That is the secret to having JOY.....how do we attain joy? It is when you channel your happiness from the outside in; therefore, creating what I call a chemical reaction with our hormones that releases JOY from within the depths of our soul.

If you don't believe that is true, let's try the reverse effect removing the joy....unhappiness creates stress that causes your body to release toxins that make you sick; therefore, creating a state of depression. Wow, where is the happiness? Where is the Joy? I will tell you how to get your happiness back, start smiling, laughing, and enjoying yourself; and your joy will be restored, healing the body. Therefore, if someone is stealing your happiness, you need to start developing an AVOID strategy.

72nd Type of Person to Avoid

Avoid People Who Try To Oppress You

Why is it that as soon as we overcome one obstacle, another one follows? Obstacles are designed to keep us consumed, blind, blocked, or divided. If we do not find a way to recognize the obstacle for what it is, while putting it in its proper perspective, it will consume us with the mind-blocking

Chapter 15 | Ruby Fleurcius

actions, reactions, or thoughts that are attached to it. We will find that obstacles do not come alone; they come with their cousins called depression, oppression, and anxiety that attaches and feeds on our negative emotions that will cause us to implode or explode with unexplainable mental and physical sicknesses or diseases.

How can we overcome depression, oppression, or anxiety? Acknowledgment is the first step to overcoming anything. If that is how we are feeling, acknowledge it, develop a plan not to feel that way, give it to God through the power of prayer. If we need to grieve then do so…it is necessary for the human psyche to move on mentally or emotionally after some form of loss, and then move on physically.

Denial suppresses and deepens our state of depression, oppression, and anxiety; therefore, making us extra sensitive, controlling, manipulative, or emotionally overbearing. As a matter of fact, it will also keep us on an emotional rollercoaster ride depending on what's going on in our lives at the time. I have found that the quickest way to get out of a depressive, oppressive, or anxious state is to laugh—it is hard to be happy and sad at the same time.

I make it my business to have an equal balance of serious and fun moments in my life to break the monotony of pumping out wisdom or doing business all the time—with my family; I am just ME. I do not pretend to be more than who I am, I laugh, I have fun, I speak country, and I crack jokes—that's what they know, and that's what they expect from me until we have a situation that requires me to put on my spiritual or business hat. I still live a normal life like everyone else; do I get upset with my family members? Absolutely! Do I allow my emotions to cause me to treat them any differently? Absolutely NOT! I live by certain standards, and I treat everyone with love, respect, and outright integrity even if I do not agree with their behavior. However, when I do business, I operate in reverse order—I put my personal life on the backburner, and handle my business, taking the emotions of my personal life out of the equation. I only deal with the business emotions at hand to ensure that my personal and professional life do not overlap.

Now, in order to operate in that fashion, we must get an understanding of how our emotions work; our emotions must choose a positive or negative state by remaining neutral, by having a positive response, or by having a negative response. Our emotions will choose one of the three, or an interchangeable combination of the three emotions which produces what we often call roller-coaster emotions. However, we must know what we are feeling in order to deal with our emotions appropriately to control certain types of behaviors, reactions, actions, or certain disrespectful things from coming out of our mouth. We do not have to think about what's positive or what's negative; our conscience already knows right from wrong—when we are doing the right thing we know it and when we are doing the wrong thing we know it as well. We can't go wrong with clean hands and a pure heart.

If we are depressed, oppressed, or anxious due to our own actions, reactions, or behaviors, then we need to make it our business to right a wrong, forgive ourselves, give it to God, and move on. It is time for you to smile your way to the top by thinking positive thoughts, doing what you enjoy doing, counteracting the negative with a positive, and creating a win-win situation out of everything.

Chapter 15 | *Ruby Fleurcius*

73rd Type of Person to Avoid

Avoid People Who Try To Steal Your Joy or Happiness

How can you find inspiration to get out of the dumps? I would say prayer helps; but it may not always give us the immediate lift needed, especially when our faith is being tried. I have found that if we find something to laugh or smile about, it will naturally take an individual out of a dark place. Better yet, we can find an inspirational song or story to bring us mentally or emotionally out of a not so great place. In my opinion, if we focus on the things we enjoy doing, we are better able to deal with, and inspire ourselves not to go mentally, emotionally, or physically into places that deplete our source of inspiration.

It is our responsibility to deal with our issues, and it is also our responsibility to safeguard our mental, emotional, and physical state of being. Now, for our spiritual state of being, this is where prayer comes in to produce a safety net for the things that we know not or do not understand. In so many words, we must do our part in bringing joy into our lives, and God will do His—it's not fair to expect God to give us what we are not willing to give to ourselves. Take a moment to embrace the people, places, and things that bring joy to your heart, while you lift your prayers on High—allowing your

Heavenly Father to align and safeguard that in which you have made the choice to embrace.

Joy takes place from within a person and happiness is a result of what takes place on the outside of a person. Never expect a relationship to make you happy, but if someone is taking the happiness that you have from you—arrange for their exit out of your life. You must be happy prior to going into a relationship with someone. If you are not, being miserable will become your middle name. You cannot expect anyone to do what you are not willing to do for yourself. Find a way to put a smile on your face.

What can a smile do for you, when you have nothing to smile about? I would definitely say that a smile can do more for us than a frown ever will. I have found that it's hard for me to stay mad or sad when I have a smile on my face or when I laugh. As a matter of fact, a simple smile can brighten someone's darkest day, if they allow it to do so; however, I have also found that laughter releases endorphins, strengthens our heart and relieves us of stress. If we pay attention, we will find that a smile will come automatically when we laugh, but when we simply smile, a laugh does not come automatically; therefore, making laughter more powerful.

I am not saying to mock or pick on others for the sake of laughing, all I am saying is that if we allow laughter to become our therapy, it will bring healing and joy to our weary hearts, while putting a smile on our face. As Proverbs 17:22 says, "A joyful heart is good medicine, but a crushed spirit dries up the bones." In my opinion, families, friendships, or relationships that laugh and pray together, stay together longer than the ones that do not; besides, if we find a way to incorporate laughter into our day, we can never use the excuse that we have nothing to smile about. Allow laughter to become your medicine to change the chemistry of your day, as well as the chemistry in all of your relationships, while becoming healthier at the same time.

74th Type of Person to Avoid

Avoid People Who Try To Keep You From Living The Good Life

In order to live the good life so to speak, we have to choose it. As I have journeyed through life, I have found that we create the life that we desire to live mentally first, through our mindset. If we think that we have it made, we will! If we think that our lives are a living nightmare, then it will become just that! Rich or poor, successful or unsuccessful, college degree or no degree, we have a say so in whether we live a good life or a nightmare. We definitely become what we think about all the time; like attracts like, and the list goes on. However, it all boils down to our thought process and our perception; therefore, we cannot blame anyone for the end result of what takes place in our lives.

Bad things happen to good people, and good things happen to bad people; however, that does not mean that we cannot have a good life because things happen. Life is very fickle; but I will say this, if we think or say that we are a loser, our life will follow that pattern. Regardless of how much money we have, regardless of how many degrees we have, or regardless of who or what we have or know, we will subconsciously find a way to prove ourselves to be correct according to the thermostat that we have set in our mind. In so many words, our lives are forced to regulate to the condition of our mindset, even if we get lucky or get a big break in life. The lottery is a prime example of this philosophy: a person can win millions of dollars, yet spend every dime of it within a few years, losing everything. Why? It is the mindset—we must change the way in which we think. Now, on the other side of this, we have someone that is rich, but they hoard every dime—they cannot live a fulfilled life because their mindset is stuck on who is trying to swindle money out of them. They have money, but they can't live a good life due to the fact that they think that everyone is up to no good.

Living in fear of losing creates a Mind Germ within one's self that places this individual on a losing streak with people leaving them lonely and destitute from within. In my opinion, if we can find a way to understand and own the fact that we are indeed a miracle, we attract miracles, and our life is full of miracles, blessings and goodness will begin to surround us in ways that we could never imagine. We are the life that keeps on giving, and if we are sharing goodness, living in goodness, and thinking good thoughts—the Law of Reciprocity has to bring it back into our lives. For example, if a man asks us for water, we must give him water out of the goodness of our heart, expecting nothing in return; therefore, goodness along with favor has to come back to us in our time of need. But, if a man asks for water and we laugh, giving him nothing when we are empowered to do so, or we give in vinegar for water, we have just caused the Law of Reciprocity to bring back in full-circle the seed that we have sown.

Along with the mindset of goodness, our actions and reactions must become good as well—we cannot live by a double-standard of being good to certain people, and neglecting others. Just remember that sowing goodness is a prerequisite to continue living the good life, and the moment we change our mind on goodness, it will withhold its reward. Living the good life is within your reach, and it is your responsibility to extract the good out of all that you do, say, and become.

CHAPTER 16

Roaring Truth

Can you really love someone you don't know or have never met? Although some would say, "yes"—my answer is "NO!" In my opinion, when dealing with relationships, we must bond mentally, physically, emotionally, and spiritually—if we have not come into physical contact with a person, we are going to miss something. We can certainly care about someone, as well as his or her well-being, or maybe even to fill a temporary void; nevertheless, love is a little different.

I have found that most often we confused love with infatuation because we allow our feelings to override our sense of judgment. When we cannot see, feel, or touch someone, our mind will create an image of what we desire; and, most often our desires are centered around power, money, and sex. As a matter of fact, it is our mental perception that causes our mind to create a mental picture of superficial love; and, once we remove those elements of power, money, and sex out of the equation, we will find that the conditions of our infatuation will change quickly. If left unchecked, our infatuation will turn into resentment, hate, or repulsiveness when we are rubbed the wrong way.

Now, on the other hand, real love is unconditional—if we are able to be around someone without power/status/fame, without having a dime in their pocket, without having sex with them, we will find that we will begin to have a longer lasting relationship of substance that will turn into love. I am not saying that we must become blinded by love, or to settle for less. All I am saying is to be true to thyself about who and what we love, without allowing our infatuation to place us in a position that will compromise our integrity or our purpose.

When we are able to truly love ourselves first, we are better able to love and let go, exercise tough love, love freely, or place limits on what may cause a derailment in our lives. Furthermore, if an unconditional friendship is not developed before the infatuation wears off, it's possible that the relationship will soon feel like a prison sentence; especially, when dealing with this new wave of cyber love, cyber cheating, and cyber sexting. Make sure that infatuation is not getting the best of you—plus, if you have not experienced at least 4 seasons with someone to feel the ups and downs in a relationship, beware! With every season change will come—if you have not been through the seasons together, you can rest assured once the newness wears off, your eyes will be opened to reality!

75th Type of Person to Avoid

Avoid People Who Are Emotionally Exhausting

It is imperative that you master your emotional tongue opposed to allowing your emotional tongue to master you. An emotional tongue is basically speaking out of emotion. Yes, it happens to the best of us, and no, this does not apply to the women only. Men are just as emotional as women; they just know how to cover up their emotions a little better than women. This is not a man or woman thing; this is a reality thing of what's mastering you. Emotions that are not dealt with properly could lead to missed opportunities caused by unintentional self-sabotage. How do you prevent this? It's real simple, think before you speak and ask the Holy Spirit to guide your tongue.

Sandpaper emotions will always cause people to rub you the wrong way. Regardless of whether you are rubbed the wrong way or not, listed below are 2 Emotional No-Nos:

1. Never make decisions when you are emotionally imbalanced.
2. Never manipulate people by becoming emotional.

We are all a little rough around the edges in some area of our lives; however, reacting inappropriately will cause us to lose more than we will ever gain. So, watch out for the

temper! Giving a person, place, or thing control over our emotions will always keep us in a state of disarray or on an emotional roller-coaster.

It only takes a few seconds to pray before you react. If you don't know what to pray for—just say, "Help me, Lord" or "Holy Spirit, take over." Don't waste your precious time fighting against yourself, the things that cause you pain, or the things that you don't want. Conflict is designed so that you can take the negative energy, and turn it into something positive.

Today, relax and focus on the things that you do want, to ensure that you are able to smooth out those rough edges. Seek peace in all that you do and chaos will find its way out of your life; granting you a double-portion of your blessing for not giving up. No matter what's going on in your life, control your emotions.

76ᵗʰ Type of Person to Avoid

Avoid People Who Are Undisciplined

When we lack discipline in our lives, we will become a slave to something. I have zero tolerance for excuses, and I have my reasons. Discipline, happens to be another big one for me as well—I know we all have our own vices; however, we must find a way to bring whatever it is under subjection to

Chapter 16 | Ruby Fleurcius

bring ourselves out of bondage to safeguard our lineage. If we don't master discipline by this stage in the game, we are doomed to become reckless mentally, emotionally, spiritually, and physically.

There are some things that money will not be able to buy as far as our mental, emotional, and spiritual well-being. In my opinion, that's the worst type of enslavement that one could ever endure. We are a slave to something—although we deny it—we are a slave to Food, Cellphones, Television, Social Media, Sex, Money, Power, Cheating, Friends with Benefits, Smoking, Drinking, Drugs, etc. That is our reality—it is a form of enslavement, and we cannot see it as such.

The best way I have found to break free of our bondage is to sit under great leadership and become mentored by them. Environmental conditioning has caused more setbacks than we could care to imagine; therefore, making mentoring extremely important when trying to build quality relationships. However, one must remember, each leader has their own set of rules; and, if you don't learn them, you will become defeated because your rules will not work on another man's territory—you never enter another man's territory unequipped or uncharted—do your homework. If you don't learn his rules, and his game; along with your rules, and your game; that are backed up by God's rules, and God's game with a well-developed **STRATEGY**—you are going to be defeated every single time! If you are going to run with the **BIG BOYS**, you have to learn how to think like them. It's time out for the cat and mouse, tit for tat games—this is a **GOD RULED NATION**. There is a certain order that is set in place, and you need to learn it! It tells you that on the Dollar Bill—In God, We Trust; however, that is also why we call the Dollar Bill currency—you have to keep it moving. Spreading, passing it along, sharing, giving, paying it forward, reciprocity, etc., that is the only way you can break a limitation! **Be Warned!** Be careful what you spread—make sure it is goodness, to ensure goodness is coming back to you. Because if you are spreading ill-will, that same Law of Reciprocity is in effect as well. Oh, by the way, make sure you develop a good strategy and not a scheme; schemes have a tendency to backfire on those who are concocting ill-will, especially against God's chosen ones. I am sharing this information for you to do good, and not evil.

77ᵗʰ Type of Person to Avoid

Avoid People Who Do Not Embrace Opportunity

Insecurity causes the best of us to become the worst at being receptive to others with bright, new, and innovative ideas that will benefit us for the better. All too often, people reject the great ideas of others, simply because they do not feel as if they were smart enough, creative enough, or whatever enough to come up with a solution or idea themselves. So, they just outright reject what others have to offer. It is best that we do not become a part of the naysayers. If we recognize a great idea, embrace it. If someone is a great inspiration, embrace it. If someone has a great point-of-view, embrace it. If someone does something great or looks great, compliment him or her. Life is too short to reject the greatness of others—it is through their greatness that we are able to shine brightly. Just remember, the greatest inspiration, idea, or concept will come when you least expect it and most often from a person, place, or thing that you would never expect it from.

There are going to be events or circumstances that may appear difficult; yet, don't waste time twiddling your thumbs—you must take action when necessary. Standing still is not an option when the right opportunity comes knocking at your door. Quick question, "When opportunity knocks, what will you do?" Will you open the door or leave it closed? Before you answer this question, you must exercise caution—every opportunity will not be the RIGHT opportunity. Well, how do you know when the right opportunity comes? You will be fully prepared for it! Preparation is the key to open the door when the right opportunity presents itself to you. There is no limit to what you can achieve; so, don't be afraid to soar beyond the horizon. It's already yours, so you might as well become relentless about it! The determination to soar beyond the call will bring out the champion inside of you, and it begins with you imagining yourself succeeding at whatever you do.

78th Type of Person to Avoid

Avoid People Who Despitefully Use You

When someone takes your kindness as a weakness, you must put distance between the two of you. Most of the time, we are used, misused, or deceived all in the name of love; and, until we understand what's taking place, we will continue to be used by those who prey on our weaknesses. That's why there is so much fraud over the internet, women looking for love, men looking for love—we are looking for something that we are not getting at home. We label it as "Killing Time." Come on…it's called filling a void—it is that void that makes us vulnerable.

79th Type of Person to Avoid

Avoid People Who Are A Copycat

When someone only wants to be your friend for ideas, concepts, or wisdom without putting back into the pot, they must be put on the AVOID list, unless you enjoy being used. There are some people that befriend others to simply highjack their ideas.

How do you deal with the lack of creativity? In my

opinion, we must deal with the lack of creativity diligently. When we find ourselves piggy-backing off the creativity of others, it is a tell-tale sign that we are blocked in some way, shape, or form; although, we all have a creative side. Not all are able to understand it, or are willing to use it for that matter. Our creativity requires exercise; if not, it will lay dormant, allowing us to create our own limits that will keep us from achieving the desires of our heart. If we are able to recognize the creativity in others, surely we are able to recognize it in ourselves as well. All we need to do is work on or exercise our creativity every day, because the only limits that we will ever have during this journey through life are the ones we place upon ourselves.

Go ahead and get those creative juices flowing by praying for your own creativity. Besides, it brings a sense of joy that plagiarism, the copy-cat syndrome, or riding on someone else's creativity could never give you; and, one would not have to live with the constant thought of being found out. Not only that, you can't go wrong doing your own creative thing, especially if it's a God-given talent.

Once this is understood, courage will begin to open the doors of opportunity, and close the doors of deceitful ones; therefore, causing you to take action, take risks, make mistakes, etc. and most of all, it will provide you with great opportunities to succeed against all odds. Courage is always on your side, for the simple fact that you do what you do because you are blessed to do it!

80th Type of Person to Avoid

Avoid People Who Criticize You

Avoid those who sit back and criticize others for doing what they cannot do at all, what they are not willing to do, or doing what they are not gifted to do.

If you learn how to avoid the critic or tune them out, it will help keep you from jumping from one thing to the next. I have found that the lack of focus or the fear of criticism is quite common in those who are not setting goals at all, or those who set goals and for some reason or another do not achieve them. When setting a goal, we must draw a roadmap on how we are going to execute our plan of action and then develop a step-by-step system on how we see our plan working for us. Remember, unwise decisions or unplanned goals will keep us running from one thing to the next; or better yet, one person to the next.

People, places, and things come into our life out of need or greed; and, mapping our goals out will help make sense of what we see in our head. Take a moment to put your goals on paper—it doesn't matter whether it's a relationship goal, success goal, promotion goal, finance goal, business goal, etc. This will help you weigh the pros and the cons before making a permanent decision regarding something or someone that's designed to be temporary.

81st Type of Person to Avoid

Avoid People Who Do Not Communicate

Communication is all around us! If someone refuses to communicate, it breaks down the relationship automatically. We stimulate each other through conversation; and if we are not talking, we cannot express ourselves effectively. Here on planet Earth, we need that eye contact, and that slight nod from time-to-time, confirming that we are listening to the ones we claim to love. This will definitely help us streamline our selfishness to better avail ourselves to be a great friend, mother, father, lover, partner, husband, wife, etc.

Your best bet is to always keep it real with the people you love, and never think that you are too good or too whatever for them. Try to help everyone within reason, because there are enough blessings to go around, and you never know where your next blessing will come from or who may bless you.

Listen to me and listen to me well, whatever you want out of life is not going to happen by chance, it is going to happen by CHOICE. Don't be afraid to have a heart to heart conversation with God before you speak with anyone else about your relationship, your goal, your situation, your circumstance, or your outcome. As of today, start making wise choices while refusing to compromise your integrity. And, watch how God's promises come to you, naturally as the windows of opportunity swing wide open.

82nd Type of Person to Avoid

Avoid People Who Take Your Kindness For A Weakness

People will try you to see how much they can get away with….such as life. If you recognize game in advance, go ahead and part ways before you run into some serious problems. This person will always be on the lookout for ways to get-over on you, BEWARE.

Why do we have weak spots? It doesn't matter how strong we may appear, we all have weak spots—some more than others, but we all have them. Now, the difference in the ones who appear strong, they learn how to cover up their weaknesses, or they learn how to work through them. On the other hand, we have those who simply don't care about their weak spots; they let everything hang out, and they do not care about who or what their weaknesses are affecting. Just remember that an unresolved or overlooked weak spot will always bring its cousin **déjà vu** along…..so beware. In so many words, if history keeps repeating itself regarding a situation, circumstance, or event—it's time to take a look from within. In my opinion, vultures can spot our weaknesses a mile away; and, that is exactly why they wait around to prey on the weak, the naive, the sheltered, the ones who are not street smart/street savvy, and the ones that are blind to their own reality. Consequently, it is this type of unchecked or unrealized behavior that contributes to the long list of mental, physical, emotional, spiritual, and occasional abuse, even if we don't like to admit it. From now on, I need you to focus on you. The answer to all of your questions lies within your very own soul—everything you need is within your reach......stretch yourself, and you will find the hidden treasures or answers that you are looking for.

83rd Type of Person to Avoid

Avoid People Who Embarrass You In Public

Public humiliation is a big NO-NO! What goes on in your house should stay in your house. Once you bring your business into the public eye, it then becomes everyone's business. If you are in relations with a person that's humiliating you publicly, and you are okay with that—then one must really wonder what's going on from within. THAT'S NOT CUTE!

Why do people mistreat others? There are various reasons why people do what they do; however, the most common reasons are jealousy, envy, conditioning, peer-pressure, or the mirror-effect of how we are being treated by that particular individual or environment. For whatever reason we are mistreating others or being mistreated by others, it doesn't justify having a bad attitude. For me, that is one of the biggest turn-offs regardless of the situation, circumstance, event, or who that person may or may not be. Furthermore, if we do not possess the desires of our heart, we must check our attitude first—it will definitely inform us of our disposition in life. I always say, "When you don't know, you just don't know!"

In all reality, there are some people who really don't know how to treat others—actually, being nice, cordial, and polite feels really weird to them. When we are brought up in an environment of utter maltreatment or chaos, we become accustomed to that way of living—until we learn, or are exposed to a different way of living. Just because we are exposed to a better way of living, doesn't mean that we will change automatically; we must make a conscious and consistent effort to become better or to simply live better. In my opinion, once we learn how to treat ourselves better, our way of living becomes better, and we will begin to treat others better as well.

If this doesn't happen as we become aware of who we are and how we are living, the reverse effect will begin to take place when we least expect it. The most common reverse effect is as follows: If we treat others poorly, our lives will begin to spiral out of control, and then the self-critic will begin to beat our self-esteem to a mere pulp. In the end, we will begin to wallow in our sorrows unless we do something about it. Seeing a psychiatrist may help, but until we are willing to help ourselves, we are indeed fighting a losing battle if we continue to mistreat others for whatever reason. It will not cost you anything to be nice and courteous to yourself and others. I firmly believe that you are in control of your destiny, please don't allow the mistreatment of others to prevent you from having and enjoying the desires

Chapter 16 | Ruby Fleurcius

of your heart. Lastly, having love in your heart will take you much further than hate ever will, GUARANTEED!

84th Type of Person to Avoid

Avoid People Who Avoid You

Do not chase someone who does not want to be bothered— find something else to do. Do not appear so desperate or weak! It is a TURN OFF. Desperation makes you an EASY catch for trash. Make sure you never beg for love; it will have to come naturally, they either feel it for you or they do not. Clingy people usually suffocate a relationship because people really need their space!

God forbid if you have suffered a broken heart behind being avoided; but, I have found that when our heart is broken, that's more of a reason to listen to it. Our heart will tell us things that our emotions override based on our sense of vulnerability. Once we are able to get our emotions in check, we are then able to hear what our heart is saying— until then, we will find ourselves wallowing in things that our heart is trying to heal from. If we take the time to put our emotions on the backburner, we are then able to allow our heart to heal.

If you are wallowing in something, simply take a moment to pray about your emotions first and then the situation or circumstance that caused it, and put that individual on the AVOID list.

85th Type of Person to Avoid

Avoid People Who Laugh At You

If someone does not recognize or laugh about the great person that you are, hit the avoid button!   However, that does not give one an excuse not to work on SELF…..

Why is our worth not recognized by others? Oh boy, this is a catch 22 question—so let me tread very carefully. This could happen for many different reasons, but the most common reasons would be that we do not recognize our own worth, people have lost faith in our worthiness, we are too emotional, how we are presenting our worth, or we are an undercover hypocrite.   When we are not true to ourselves, we know it, and others can see it, regardless of how we try to cover it up. In my opinion, if we are worthy of something or someone, we do not have to try too hard to show off—all we have to do is simply walk in it and our gift will make room for us.

Whether you have stopped believing in you, whether people have stopped believing in you, or whether you have become lost in the pain, the trials, or the chaos of life, you must look from within for your strength. It does not matter what or who you try—it's like **déjà vu**. Your life will repeat the same issues until you finally take the time out to focus on your inner self, to create some **vujá dé** in your life. This means to change your whole perspective or how you view everything. Trust me, if you can do this, I promise you that you will have the last laugh, guaranteed.

86th Type of Person to Avoid

Avoid People Who Pretend Like They Know Everything

How would someone handle a chauvinist who thinks that he or she is always right? It's very simple—every man appears to be right in his or her own eyes; therefore, it is better not to tell a chauvinist that he or she is wrong, just agree and proceed. Actually, agree and proceed is one of the most effective techniques in sales. When we disagree with someone who gloats on their superiority, that is an indication that their mind is already made up. There is no need for us to try to disagree with them, unless we are looking for conflict. I am not saying that a chauvinist is always right; all I am saying is that if we want to communicate effectively with a chauvinist, we must make them feel as if they are right. If you happen to run into a chauvinist, simply agree and proceed in the conversation without outright disagreeing with them, and watch how he or she will begin to open up to you.

87th Type of Person to Avoid

Avoid People Who Overlook You on Purpose

Never let them see you sweat. Stay calm and don't freak out about the big or small things. Controlling your emotions will help you control your attitude and actions, to enable you to deal with issues that tend to come out of nowhere. Most often, people overlook others when they cannot get some form of instant gratification. The fly-by-night gratification has a way of impeding our progress especially when we need it the most. The desire for uncontrollable instant gratification could possibly cost us more than we are willing or even able to pay, especially when the people we love are involved. Of course, instant gratification often goes unnoticed to those who are getting what they want; however, the more it goes unnoticed, the more we want, and the easier it will become to overlook the faults that contribute to our digressions and/or regressions in life. In my opinion, the only limits that we have are the ones we place upon ourselves, so progression and avoiding those who overlook you are a must, if we want to truly become the person that we are created to be.

As long as you know what you are dealing with, don't allow them to get the satisfaction of knowing that they may have offended you. Keep a straight face and **NEVER**

ALLOW A TEAR TO FALL FROM YOUR FACE. If you have a moment of weakness, do it in your own space, behind closed doors—you may bend, but do not break.

88ᵗʰ Type of Person to Avoid

Avoid People Who Cringe When You Show Up

If someone cringes as if your presence is repulsive, you need to find an exit quickly. There is no need to brown-nose; if one is not accepted in a certain circle, shake the dust off your feet and keep it moving.

When we feel blessed, or when we begin to live a well-to-do life, it's so easy to get caught up in bragging about what we have, do, say, and experience while forgetting about certain classes of people or cringing when they are round as if we are better than them. This should not be so.....we are blessed to be a blessing, and we should love thy neighbor as thyself. We should hold ourselves to a higher standard, but we dare not look down on others for their standards.

The art of our true success is based on the biblical principle of seed, time, and harvest; and, for that reason, we must plant our seeds of blessings in our time of harvest to ensure that our blessings remain. I firmly believe that living life is no joke, and it's a shame to allow an unused or misused blessing, gifts, or calling to fall by the wayside. Embrace the art of successful living by learning how to motivate others through your wisdom, creativity, ambitions or skills without allowing bragging or boasting to clout your end-result.

89ᵗʰ Type of Person to Avoid

Avoid People Who Play Games

Relationship greed has contributed to the games of love since the beginning of time. At one point men played most of the games; but now, women are holding their own in this arena as well. The cat and mouse relationship games are contributing to the downfall of real love.

Avoid people who are greedy in a relationship. A person already has an idea of what they want from you and how to get it. Now it's up to you to know what it is. No more excuses about they don't know what they want—they do! Most often, if someone says that they don't know what they want—this is a sign that they are **UNAVAILABLE**, but they want to be greedy for the fear of losing out!

Break free of the game; if someone leaves you for another person, don't try to win them back or sabotage their relationship with someone else—that's childish. Don't ignore the obvious signs; respectfully, MOVE ON. It may hurt to lose; your ego may be bruised; but trust me, it was only a matter of time before they moved on anyway. However, if a relationship is meant to be, they will come back on their own, if that's what one desire to happen. If not, cut the cord completely.

Sharing someone intimately with another person is a quick way to set ourselves up for hurt. If they are not ready to commit; and they love the game more than the relationship, then our best bet is to keep moving—being emotionally committed to two or more people at the same time is dangerous and unhealthy. In order to avoid such atrocity, it's best to step away from a situation as such and keep yourself busy. There is no need to sit around waiting on a relationship when you can develop a relationship with oneself and make your life more productive until the right one for you comes along.

90th Type of Person to Avoid

Avoid People Who Secretly Wish For Your Demise

If someone wishes you ill-will, leave them alone....you do not need any bad blood in your environment. Avoid them at all cost—this type of person will hurt you.

Doing the right thing for the wrong reason is just as bad as outright doing the wrong thing in itself. We as individuals must take into account what we are thinking or doing and the reasons why. How often do we make choices difficult?

More than we care to imagine, right? Our decision-making process is essential in the way in which we would like to reap the fruits of our labor. Most often, we do not make a choice because we have not really made up our mind about something or someone. Of course, choices do become difficult, especially when we are confused about what we want or do not want in our lives; and, even more confusing when there is a bad habit involved. However, bad habits can become good if we know and understand the underlying reason that the habit became bad in the first place.

The right mental attitude is by far the way to go when you are on top of your game or when your game is on top of you. When you combine your positive thoughts with the Mind of God, there is no limit on what you can or cannot do.

91st Type of Person to Avoid

Avoid People Who Secretly or Openly Compete Against You

A competitive spirit is an obvious sign of insecurity. When your game is tight, you do not have to compete with others against your own uniqueness. Therefore, if you find your niche, and master it—you will not have to really compete, you will just have to get a little creative or strategic. That is the difference! However, if you have someone all in your chops trying to steal your ideas to out do you with your own stuff—that is outright PIRACY! Nevertheless, it happens to me all the time—I am accustomed to it now. As a matter of fact, I use my ideas as a gauge to see who I can trust and who I cannot. With my personality, I am extremely nice and humble; but, I also strategically appear weak to draw out the wolves in sheep's clothing. As my trump card, I will place half of the idea on the table, or I will give them just enough information to betray me. Is it a game....No. This is BUSINESS. When doing business, you need to know who you are dealing with; if not—you will look very UNWISE competing against someone with your own idea! I have been there before, and it's embarrassing to become surpassed with your own idea. Protect yourself.

How can we spot an insecure person? That is simple, just look around—we are all insecure about something. However, an extremely insecure person can be spotted by their jealousy/envy of others, their extreme ability to brow-beat others, their ability to criticize others about the same things that they are guilty of, their ability to profusely gossip about others, their ability to use the past against others as leverage to get what they want, their ability to be insensitive to the feelings/emotions of others, and their ability to abuse others mentally, physically, emotionally or spiritually without giving it a second thought. Insecurity causes one to look for weaknesses in others to actually hide or cover up our very own hidden weaknesses.

If you want to become secure, simply start looking for the good in everyone, and watch how the natural goodness begins to rise up out of you. Besides, there will not be a reason to compete with someone else.

92nd Type of Person to Avoid

Avoid People Who Treat You Like A Doormat

When a person walks all over you simply because they can is very disrespectful on their behalf; and, you need to avoid them. Why does a nice person get treated like a doormat? It's hard to say, but some people are not accustomed to nice people. When someone lacks enthusiasm for us, they will begin to treat us as if we do not matter.

The lack of enthusiasm has a way of bringing about discontentment, complaining, and hatefulness that causes the desires of our heart to elude us. For example, if we are not enthused about our mate, our relationship will become strained; therefore, leaving room for someone else to capture his or her attention. If we are not enthused about our job, we will tend to make unnecessary mistakes, or create a hostile environment for others. I can come up with all types of examples; however, it doesn't make a difference what I say if we are grumpy about life in itself; besides, who wants to be with or live with a person who makes his or her life miserable. As the Book of Proverbs 21:9 tells us, "It is better to dwell in a corner of the housetop, than with a brawling woman in a wide house." In my opinion, whatever we are not enthused about will begin to lose its value as time passes on and the newness wears off. Therefore, in order to build great relationships, you must make it your business to become enthusiastic about something or someone that may have been deprived of the right to truly enjoy the great person that you are. If you are the one that's being deprived, then one must evaluate the situation accordingly to resolve it or begin to concoct an exit strategy.

93rd Type of Person to Avoid

Avoid People Who Vex Your Spirit

When our spirit becomes vexed when we are around someone, we need not ignore it. A person with a calm spirit will chase away a confrontational spirit, and a confrontational person will drive away those who are adamant about keeping a calm environment.

When our spirit becomes vexed, we must mentor ourselves with the Fruits of the Spirit; therefore, it becomes very hard to go wrong in our way. Although, we all come from a diverse background, and we all are somewhat a byproduct of our environment; however, when we allow the Fruits of the Spirit to govern us—our integrity will stand regardless of where we came from or what we have been through. Do you remember when the 10 spies came back with a bad report, and Joshua and Caleb did not fall into that trap—that's what I am speaking of right now. Regardless, of what anyone says, practice the Good Report of Love, Joy, Peace, Patience, Kindness, Goodness, Faithfulness, Gentleness, and Self-control—trust me; you will touch places in a person's heart that they did not know existed. That is a promise that I will make to you—if you exercise the Fruits of the Spirit when mentoring yourself, as well as those who are in need of what you have to offer.

It does not matter if they try to pass judgment, it does not matter if they try to find fault, and it does not matter if they try to set a trap for you—you will still be able to reach them regardless. It will be through your imperfections that they will see the Glory of God work. Trust me on that one! For it is truly through my imperfections that I can pull such powerful information to bring forth to help an imperfect World.

94th Type of Person to Avoid

Avoid People Who Will Not Help You

This is a great way to see who is for you and who is not! However, if you are in need and the ones that proclaim to love you will not help you, it may be a possibility that God is trying to open your eyes to reality. This is not just about money; this is about the simple things in life.......when life has given you a few lemons to make lemonade.

How do you handle being on the losing end of the deal?

I often say what appears as a loss, maybe a blessing in disguise. We have become accustomed to having the people, places, and things that we want, while at the same time losing focus on our needs. We are conditioned to look down on the needy, therefore forgetting about the wanty. What is wanty? A wanty is a person who wants everything—they also have other titles such as high-maintenance, gold-diggers, etc. and they will do almost anything to get what they want, or do almost anything not to appear like a loser. Now, after understanding a wanty person, being needy is not so bad after all. Nevertheless, we all have wants and needs—in order to filter between the two, loss must take place in our lives whether we like it or not.

There are times when we all feel as if we are on a winning or losing streak; however, we must understand that there will be times when we lose to win and win to lose. For me, when I lose, I consider it my pruning season with an understanding that no good thing will be withheld from me. When we believe that we are a winner from within, we become a magnet to winning, or if we think that we are a loser from within, we become that.

In order to maximize your full potential, it's imperative that you focus on the people, places, and things that you need in your life, and allow the "Lose to win" attitude to permeate through your very own soul. This will allow all things to work together for your good, especially if you prepare yourself to win mentally, physically, emotionally, and spiritually—it's your birthright anyway.

95ᵗʰ Type of Person to Avoid

Avoid People Who Refuse To Mentor Others

We as a generation must prepare our youths for a transfer of wisdom, knowledge, and power to carry on our legacy; therefore, producing a continuous cycle of great relationships. We cannot be afraid to transfer the power, vision, and hope into ourselves or successors—we are required to give back! The Law of Reciprocity is a prerequisite for those who desire to reap the harvest and keep the harvest of the fruits of our labor. Hoarders are not allowed to keep the promises of the seeds of the sower—our harvest is meant to be shared.

If it takes you to get you some apprentices, do just that! A little bit goes a long way—you never know the lives that you may inspire by small acts of kindness. It may take years to see the benefits, but trust me it is well worth it. It brings me joy every time I hear a personal testimony of how I inspired someone when they were just a little child; although, I wasn't trying to get any brownie points—I was just being the natural person that I am. However, it brings tears of joy, to see a child go on to become a Doctor, Lawyer, Teacher, Entrepreneur, etc. It will do the same for you as well, when those testimonies start coming back to you—it will make you want to do more, empower more, mentor more, and share more.

If you choose to become a passive mentor, occasional

mentor, or a more involved mentor—do something. If you do not empower another, the knowledge, and wisdom that one possess will cause you to implode. That is why the smartest people start breaking down psychologically, and the not so smart people prevail because they are smart enough to share what they have learned from other smart people. That behooves me; but, that is how it works! Therefore, if you learn the laws of how the system works, you too can become SMART! God has created this Universe with Laws, Systems, Strategies, Concepts, and Divine Order; and, if you can wrap your head around that—WISDOM is yours!

Listen to me, it is through this wisdom that God feeds me, that I feed you, and I expect you to digest it, and then take it and share with others. You cannot do it alone; you need a team—I have given you enough information thus far, and you should have enough to get people on your side.

96ᵗʰ Type of Person to Avoid

Avoid People Who Prevent You From Doing The Right Thing

What do you do when someone's trying to hold you back from succeeding at doing the right thing? I would definitely say, "Do the right thing anyway!" That should give us the incentive to become, see, and do more to achieve the desires of our heart. When it comes down to succeeding at doing what's right, envy has a way of creeping in to steal friendships, marriages, partnerships, etc. It is envy that causes someone to try to hold us back, oppress us, sabotage our success, speak ill-will against us, create chaos, and the list goes on.

The best thing that you could ever do for yourself is to focus on succeeding in all that you do, while the naysayers waste their time allowing envy to consume them. Our wisdom is not just for our use. Our creativity is not just for our enjoyment. Our ambitions are not of our own. Our skills are not just for our pleasure. Everything that we have is designed to encourage or bless the lives of someone else. There is no need to convince someone that you possess a certain type of creativity, wisdom, ambition, or skill—just do what you do best, help yourself, help others and allow God to do the rest. It's just that simple!

97th Type of Person to Avoid

Avoid People Who Stalk You

If someone stalks you or have the potential to stalk you, RUN! Don't entertain that relationship....in my opinion, that would be a zero tolerance issue. Nevertheless, a stalker knows how far to go, and who will allow them to get away with that type of behavior.

How much will you accept? We set the pace for how

much we will accept in our lives and how much we will not. As I look back over my life, I can recall saying under pressure, "I can't take it anymore," and I am pretty sure we all have said it at some point. However, I have come to understand that our acceptance level governs our tolerance level of what we are going through. For example, if someone knows that we have a zero-tolerance level on something, the chances of them violating our boundaries are lessened; now, on the other hand, if someone knows that we will put up with anything or we are simply a push-over, we will have mad chaos in our lives. As we very well know, our mouth can say anything, but it is our actions and reactions that really speak volume.

Today, decide in your heart what you are willing to accept and what you are not, then move forward letting others know where you stand by making the appropriate changes in your actions, and not mere words.

98th Type of Person to Avoid

Avoid People Who Refuse To Deal With Their Addictions

What do you do when a person does not help himself or herself? In my opinion, if the person we are trying to help is becoming combative, destructive, or totally rejecting what we have to offer, we may have to step back until that person wants to be helped.

When we find ourselves going against the grain with someone about something that will benefit them in the long-run, it is possible that they do not want help because his or her desires are elsewhere. When a person doesn't appreciate us or what we have to offer, we must find a way to move on to those who need us, opposed to fighting a losing battle. We cannot make a person want something or someone that they are not ready for.

Our best bet is to reach out and help those who desire and welcome your helping hand. Remember, God helps those who have a desire to help themselves; and, God also helps those who don't understand what they need as well. Although you may take a step back from them, hope for the best and God will do the rest.

99th Type of Person to Avoid

Avoid People Who Are Evil

When someone is outright evil, you know it and they know it too—they don't make it a secret. Sleeping with the enemy is not a great way to build a successful relationship; therefore, one must tread with extreme caution. Do not entertain them.....Do not entertain negativity; you must weed them out.....they will choke you.

Evil has been around since the beginning of time, and it's not going anywhere; therefore, we must learn how to be ye different! We create our own issues by allowing an open door of evil to gain entry into our lives, and we also have the power to close that open door as well. Just as nature is designed to correct itself, we are designed to self-correct as well; however, we must allow it, and we must filter out the negativity! I have found that through the power of choice and prayer, we can overcome evil, or we can overcome the things that are designed to sift, detour, or beset us. Of course, we will not become immune to negative or evil people; however, we can learn the characteristics to ensure that we are able to AVOID them.

The greatest encourager known to man is the encourager that resides within oneself. Greatness is not achieved by winging it in folly; it is achieved by having a system in place to keep us focused on the goal and not the obstacle. Living life is not about who is the most intelligent, it's about who's the most committed and who's the most focused on achieving, doing, and becoming more than what they are right now. Taking action will help you to overcome the challenges that may easily beset you from achieving your desired result or your desired goal. And, when doing so, you must answer these 3 questions:

1. "What am I trying to achieve?"
2. "What's the main objective of this achievement?"
3. "How can this achievement provide a benefit?"

Instead of being mired by defeat, get a plan and stick to it; therefore, winging it will become a thing of the past. Plus, when you know your strengths, weaknesses, skills, values, attitudes, and interests, you will become better prepared for the surprises that life may spring up on you.

Hard work will drive anyone to create their own repertoire of greatness while being mentored to the top. Who doesn't want to be great? We all do, even if we don't want to admit it. Our repertoire of greatness is within our reach as long as we are willing to work for it. As we all know, the fruits of our labor require hard work, dedication, accountability, and a positive attitude. Good potential that's not acted upon is what? An unpurposeful potential! When we find a purpose for our potential, then we are better able to govern the change of it or the redirection of the energy pertaining to it. Therefore, we must focus on being consistent and committed to what we are doing.

If you truly value what you possess from within, find a mentor or coach. They are able to fine-tune what you already have, and they will help keep you from lying to yourself. Most successful people have a coach to help them to become and remain accountable for what they are doing and what they are not doing. When we are not accountable for something, we tend to become a little lazy or we will tend to put things off. It's extremely hard to become lazy when our mentor or coach is holding us accountable for our developmental process. As we all know, we are not born with the ability to achieve peak performance; it is developed. We have a few great abilities that often go overlooked and they are:

1. Our ability to become teachable.
2. Our ability to learn.

3. Our ability to share.

God will enlarge our territory once we become learnable, teachable, and sharable; we have a great combination that could achieve anything with the proper mentoring. And, having one without the other will cause us to become limited. Who wants to work hard and have our efforts blocked for the same amount of energy? No one, of course. So, it is better to get rid of anything that has the potential of hindering our progress to ensure that we are able to maximize our abilities without squandering them.

100th Type of Person to Avoid

Avoid People Who Prevent You From Praying or Developing a Relationship With God

If someone tries to stop you from having a relationship with God, that should send up all types of red flags. If you stop yourself from praying or developing a relationship with God—that should be a red flag as well. It is imperative that you develop a spiritual relationship with God first, He is indeed the one that's going to stand beside you when people walk away from you. He is the One that's going to have mercy on your soul, when your heart is broken. He is the One that's going to give you favor, when you have been betrayed. He is the One that's going to cover you, when you can't see the enemy approaching. He is the One that's going to accept you, when people reject you. He is the One....you need Him, because when you have issues with the person that's blocking you from Him......who will you run to? Yes, it is Him—Your Heavenly Father. The Divine Order is to love God, love yourself, and then others.....if you get that out of order, in due time, you will have problems to provoke you to bring that relationship back into its proper perspective.

There are many different paths that will get us to our destination, and we must choose one. We can take the long way, the short way, or the wrong way—it's our choice. Life changing choices will cause the best of us to revamp our perspective in order to get things back on track. What do you do when your life jumps the track? It's real simple, get it back on track. Now, the challenge is, knowing how to get your life back on track. The first step to getting back on track is to know "how" and "why" you got off track in the first place. The lack of understanding can and will cause us to challenge that in which we have not taken the time to learn. Regardless of where we are in life or what we may have accomplished, we will always have choices, problems, and decisions. Once we understand our choices, problems, and decisions, we are better able to find a solution for all three to keep balance and harmony in our lives.

In building successful relationships, it's okay when you have to revamp some things in your life—it keeps you open to change. Let me tell you, anything that's worth having requires you to be flexible, to move when necessary, and be focused enough to revamp the things that most people overlook. When you find a purpose for your potential, you are better able to govern the change or the redirection of the energy pertaining to it—so, make sure that the track you are on is the right one.

CHAPTER 17

Grow Great

As we all know Newton's third law: "For every action, there is an equal or opposite reaction." God's Law: "Seed, Time, and Harvest." In my opinion, every move we make in life must be well calculated, or it may work against us. I am not saying that we must overthink issues, circumstances, or events that take place in our lives—I am saying that we must think through them using the "Relationship 80/20 Rule" to ensure that distractions are kept to a bare minimum. When we make decisions with this principle in mind, it will ensure that we do not fall victim to instant gratification that leads us in the wrong direction. As we look back over our lives, where we are now is a byproduct of the choices that we have made, and nothing will change unless we do.

Excellence cannot be bought; it is a developed attitude that's derived from a commitment to do and give your very best. If you really want to make a difference or an investment into yourself—from me to you, "COMMIT TO

EXCELLENCE!" Excellence will take you to places beyond your wildest dreams. Just remember that in the midst of your excellence, you will always have the choice to empower or to implode with the resources that you have been blessed with.

At this point, after reading this book, our relationships are no longer based upon a superficial facade; they are based upon our determination to learn more than we did the day before to create a win-win situation for all involved. Knowledge is power, and there is true power in knowledge; however, knowledge without any experience or action changes the rules to the ball game. In order to always keep the ball in our court, we must understand that learning in action is the key to wisdom; and, wisdom is the key to learning while in action. They work like **MAGIC** when they are put together, giving us the ability to retain more valuable information. When we base our success totally upon what we know and not upon learning more, we will eventually become stagnate. From my own personal experiences, stagnated success causes more undue pressure than not becoming successful at all. When this happens, it can and will seep over into other areas of our lives creating more havoc than we care to bear.

In whatever you do, always add learning into the equation to prevent yourself from becoming stuck in a rut or stuck in your own way of doing things. If you have not gotten the point by now, the more you learn, the more you grow; and the more you take action while growing, the more you can accomplish. So, regardless of how small your accomplishments may seem—I need you to continue to learn, learn, and learn some more. Hint, hint, sharing gives what you have learned power; and ACTION puts what you have learned in motion!   Even if you feel as if you are getting the short end of the deal regarding what you are destined to do, simply make some positive changes in your life, do what's right, and in the end, you will win. Guaranteed.   I am living proof of that.....I have been blessed to empower you with 100 Types of People to Avoid; and now, your destiny awaits you, so go get it and get your ROAR back!   Be Blessed and Be a Blessing to Someone Else.

Ruby Fleureius